Why is this book important, personally, for you?

★ BECAUSE it can help you know yourself—and shape your own future

★ BECAUSE it can help you to understand others better

★ AND BECAUSE, in all matters of the heart, this book can be an invaluable guide to romantic happiness.

Find out why your love interests are usually people born under certain signs. . .

Discover what characteristics draw you to that special someone, and how to sustain a meaningful relationship. . .

Learn which signs are compatible—and why, on the other hand, you may develop the closest, most intimate relationship with someone quite opposite in nature.

Read all about *you* and your lucky stars!

YOU AND YOUR LUCKY STARS

A Zodiac Guide to Dating,
Compatibility,
and
Personal Characteristics

BY BARBARA SHOOK HAZEN

GOLDEN PRESS · NEW YORK

CONTENTS

Introduction 7
ARIES: March 21-April 20 13
TAURUS: April 21-May 20 31
GEMINI: May 21-June 20 47
CANCER: June 21-July 20 67
LEO: July 21-August 21 85
VIRGO: August 22-September 22 . . 103
LIBRA: September 23-October 22 . . 121
SCORPIO: October 23-November 22 . . 139
SAGITTARIUS: November 23-December 20 . 157
CAPRICORN: December 21-January 19 . 173
AQUARIUS: January 20-February 18 . . 191
PISCES: February 19-March 20 . . . 209

INTRODUCTION

ASTROLOGY is the study of the stars as they relate to you, and to others. According to astrology, your traits and tendencies were determined
by the position of the heavenly bodies at the
time you were born. Your horoscope is a kind
of heavenly chart, a prediction of what you are
and a promise of what you may become.

When you were born, the heavens were ruled
by one of the twelve constellations in the imaginary belt of the sky called the Zodiac. These
twelve constellations are the twelve houses, or
signs, of the Zodiac. They are named according
to their shapes, starting with Aries, the Ram,
and ending with Pisces, the Fish.

The signs of the Zodiac are further subdi-
vided according to the four elements which in-
fluence them. Aries, Leo, and Sagittarius are
Fire signs; Taurus, Virgo, and Capricorn are
Earth signs; Gemini, Libra, and Aquarius are
Air signs; and Cancer, Scorpio, and Pisces are
Water signs.

7

Astrology, unlike astronomy, is not an exact scientific study of the stars. It is concerned with influences rather than facts, with possibilities rather than exact predictions. That is one positive reason for its importance—the possibilities can be changed. It is all up to you.

Astrology maintains that people born at a certain time, under a certain set of stars, are different from others—that a fiery Aries is not at all the same sort of person as an easygoing Taurus.

Skeptics laugh and say "mere fortunetelling." They ask, "Why should an Aquarian born in January be different from a Leo born in July?"

Astrologers answer: It *has* been scientifically proved that flowers and trees planted at different times of the year fare differently. If so, they argue, why not people?

Moreover, the moon is a heavenly body, and the moon's influence on people's behavior and moods, as well as on the tides, has long been known and charted. (And isn't it possible that our interest in astrology is at a peak today not only because we feel a strong need to reestablish spiritual values, but because we are truly in a Space Age, and man is actually traveling to the moon?)

Why is astrology important, personally, to you? Because it can help you know yourself and shape your own future. Astrology explains what you are. Whether you stay that way is up to you. In other words, a naturally lazy person can, with effort, do excellent work, and a fiery, hot-blooded person can learn to hold his temper. Sometimes knowing the problem and its pitfalls is half the battle.

Equally important, astrology helps you understand others better. You know you relate to people differently—that one person "bugs" you while you are instinctively drawn to another. Astrology explains why you are compatible or why you clash, and how best to bridge that gap, generation or otherwise.

Use this book not only to discover the real you, but to find out about your friends. Use it in special situations: when a parent seems to think, unfairly, that everything you do is wrong . . . when you have a falling out with a friend . . . when someone you see every day "gets your goat"—or, on the other hand, fascinates and turns you on.

Use the book to find out why your love interests are usually people born under certain signs, what characteristics draw you to that special someone, and how to sustain a meaningful relationship. Also, find out why you are sometimes intrigued by a person who isn't good for you or keeps you guessing. Finally, find out what signs are compatible—and why, on the other hand, you may develop the closest, most intimate relationship with someone quite opposite in nature. In all matters of the heart— from a fling to real, lasting love—this book can be an invaluable guide to romantic happiness if you will let it.

One thing, however, cannot be stressed too strongly. Astrology describes traits and inclinations. It is definitely *not* a philosophy of predestination, and it does not forecast the future. Astrology concerns itself with likelihood. Actual events are shaped by your characteristics under a given sign—plus other factors such as free will, environment, and effort.

Also, whether an inherent trait develops in a positive or negative way is up to you. For instance, egotism is the flip side of self-confidence, while impulsiveness is eagerness without inner control. With a bit of trying, a moody person from a strongly emotional sign can become a sensitive yet fully self-controlled individual.

In other words, your future is up to you. Astrology points out certain talents and tendencies. The stars caution you to shape up in certain ways, and to develop and expand yourself in others. They tell you a change for the better is possible, and that you are responsible for it.

Whether you believe there is "really something in it" or not is a personal matter. Even taken lightly, the study of astrology is enjoyable and profitable. And following these guide-lines is bound to help you be your best and do your thing in the best possible manner.

Yes, ours is a Space Age, and much of our thinking is scientific. Yet you may be among the many who still wish on a star, and thank your lucky stars—and keep a close personal eye on the sky.

BARBARA SHOOK HAZEN

ARIES

★ *March 21 - April 20* ★

ELEMENT: *Fire*
RULED BY: *Mars*
SYMBOL: *Ram*
KEY WORD: *Energetic*
JEWEL: *Garnet*
COLORS: *Red, Yellow, Shocking Pink;*
Clear Colors
LUCKY NUMBER: *9*
LUCKY DAY: *Tuesday*

OTHER IMPORTANT ARIENS:

Warren Beatty
Julie Christie
Harry Houdini
Jean-Paul Belmondo
Simone Signoret
Alec Guinness
Pearl Bailey
Sarah Vaughan
Rod Steiger
Omar Sharif
Charlie Chaplin
Elizabeth Montgomery
Sergei Rachmaninoff
Lionel Hampton

ARIES

GENERAL CHARACTERISTICS

ARIES is the first sign of the Zodiac. And first is what you aim to be, for you are a born go-getter. Bold, energetic action characterizes you. Your pace is swift and you are frequently impulsive. You move—and stop to think about the consequences afterwards.

Your symbol is the Ram, which is a forceful creature and one of the first signs of spring. Like him, you have boundless enthusiasm, and dash in spurts—here, there, everywhere. You have as many talents as you have interests. But you must learn to finish what you start, or you will fritter your energies away and not have enough to show for your efforts.

As an Aries, you are a born pioneer. You'll try anything once—a different camping trail, the latest fashion fad, or an exotic foreign food. You also enjoy meeting new people. Blind dates and new situations rarely throw you, and you hardly ever suffer from shyness.

You are a natural, yet understanding, leader. Other people follow your suggestions readily because you have such a convincing way of speaking.

You are both warm-hearted and full of self-confidence, which makes even strangers gravitate toward you. You always put up a good front. Even when things occasionally go badly, you hate to admit that you are unsure and afraid, and need sympathy as much as any of the other signs. You may become restless or moody, but you never brood. And when you are annoyed, your temper flares. You tend to blow up and get it all out of your system. You fight and forgive easily and without any lasting resentment.

You have strong convictions and the courage to stand up for them. You believe in protests and demonstrations, although any action you take is tempered by your fine intellect. And you always stand up for the underdog in an argument.

In your desire to keep moving, you sometimes make snap judgments and say foolish things without thinking. It is not in your basic nature to be either patient or practical. But you can acquire these qualities. And you will accomplish more, in the long run, if you let your ideas jell before surging ahead.

Your Aries enthusiasm is catching, and no

one is more outgoing or generous. By nature, you are optimistic, and you believe that people are basically good. Throughout life, your energy, ambition, and magnetic warmth will take you far. With just a little self-control, the potential is limitless.

PHYSICAL CHARACTERISTICS

ARIES people are unusually healthy and robust. You have a naturally strong constitution and an optimistic outlook on life.

Because you have excellent resistance, you are rarely sick. When you are, you are apt to be impatient and would rather fight a cold on your feet than stay in bed.

Going until you wear yourself out is your main health problem. It is important that you get plenty of rest, and relax from time to time. Also, you should exercise special care in sports, like skiing, where there is an element of danger. Accidents are apt to happen when you go too fast. Luckily, you have unusually good coordination and balance, so they don't happen often.

In looks, an Aries tends to be long-limbed and slender. Aries females have intense, come-hither expressions, and Aries males are often exceptionally masculine and forceful in their appearance.

In fashion, Ariens are born pacesetters. You have a keen sense of what's "in" and also right for you. You like clothes that are fun and a bit on the bold or bright side. You don't mind being the center of attention or in a different kind of dress from the others at a party. You have a special weakness for the far-out and for the slightly wild. And you are more attuned to the new than you are to the traditional. Aries males and females both have a flair for fashion, even if they do occasionally skimp on grooming time!

SCHOOL AND CAREER

YOUR mind is quick, and brimful of ideas. You naturally do well in school even though you aren't a grind or a dedicated scholar. A lot of homework doesn't bother you, but you are sometimes careless about the small details involved in doing it.

And you may have trouble concentrating. This is probably because you are paying attention to two things at once. Or your many outside activities may cause you to skimp on study time.

Because you love to play pranks, you may get into minor troubles from time to time. And you are more likely than others to chafe at authority. But you are a born leader—the kind who is apt to be captain of a team and on the honor roll.

With all your Arien capabilities and talents, you are bound to go far in the career you choose. (Though it may take you a while to choose it.) Fire is your element, and success your aim.

You are ambitious, and you are a natural in any position of authority. Collective work does not agree with you nearly as much as being head of the team. Moreover, you combine creativity with common sense. You not only spur others on, but add touches of originality to whatever you do.

Aries males are natural business leaders and are frequently found in the executive suite. An Aries male might be a creative director or a movie producer, or choose a political career. College president, stockbroker, and professional athlete would also appeal.

Aries females are ideal "girl Fridays." They are frequently the first women in their field, whether it's driving a taxi or building a bridge. Many career-minded Aries women make their mark in journalism, fashion, and interior decorating. And because they love to travel, many more become airline stewardesses or work in travel agencies. Whatever they do, they usually make their mark, and are popular with their co-workers besides.

MONEY

ARIENS like to have money simply because they enjoy life to the hilt and like many of the material things that money can buy. They are not, however, materialistic, and they are never stingy.

As an Aries, you are not only generous, but you are especially concerned with the needs of anyone you feel is underprivileged. (Ariens are the best choice for leading charity drives or fund-raising campaigns.)

You are honest, but if you are a typical Aries, you "can't save a penny." That's because you live for today. Besides, balancing a budget is to you a bore. Also, many of your purchases are impulse ones. Most of them are sound; only once in a while do you confuse extravagance with generosity—by splurging on a present that you can't really afford, or by going to a restaurant that is way out of line with your allowance.

But in spite of your slightly spendthrift ways,

you usually have enough money—because you are willing to work and have a good intuitive financial sense.

FUN AND LEISURE

You are a natural fighter and you have a strongly social nature. Your favorite sports demand vitality and strength. Football, wrestling, hockey, polo, and cross-country skiing would appeal to male Ariens, while females of this sign are likely to be attracted to tennis, speed swimming, and any number of other competitive team sports.

You like to read although you rarely take the time. You lean toward adventure stories and fast-moving fiction, and prefer short articles to long novels. In records, you like music with a strong beat, preferably fast and played with the volume turned up.

You delight in parties, both giving and going to them. You enjoy all kinds from big, noisy bashes to small, candlelit groups. Having people around sparks you to your liveliest humor, and you have a way of bringing others, who are more shy, out of their shells.

Finally, you are a born traveler. New scenes excite you, and you have an avid curiosity about other countries and peoples. You also have a knack for finding new excitement in your own neighborhood or city. Your eyes are always fresh and your approach is eager. And going somewhere, from a short jaunt to a long journey, gives you the change of pace your Aries nature needs.

HOME AND FAMILY

IN spite of your being away from home a lot, you have a strong sense of family. You are generally close to your parents, and any brothers and sisters you may have value your opinions and look to you for leadership. You enjoy their company, and having a firm home base means a lot to you.

On the other hand, you are occasionally headstrong and resent authority. You balk at being told what to do; you would rather figure it out for yourself. When conflicts occur, you tend to leap in, and may make more of an issue than there really is. Also, it is important that you learn to listen to others and bend a bit. Compromise is not the same thing as a cop-out, and all your stands don't need to be quite so strong.

Around your home, you are inventive and

helpful. Your room is always interesting and is usually bright, filled with accent touches or trappings from your many hobbies.

You are quick to lend a hand or share your belongings. And the door to your room is almost always open.

FRIENDSHIP

ARIENS like to have many friends, and they make excellent ones themselves. It is as easy for you to strike up a casual acquaintance as it is to keep a close friend. The same warmth and generous spirit spread to both.

Your capacity to give is limitless. And you have the ability to put yourself in another person's place. Your magnetism and vitality draw others to you, especially those who are more shy and unsure. It is hard for them to realize that you too are unsure, way down deep, and that occasionally your seeming bravado and "I don't care what anyone thinks" attitude is a cover-up for great sensitivity.

Actually, this is why you have such sympathy —you really *do* understand the other person's feelings.

Only occasionally do you tend to bully and dominate friends. You expect them to go along with your candidate, or to go to the movie you have chosen. Sometimes you are merely thoughtless, or make up your own mind so quickly you expect others to do the same. Impatience and abruptness are the pitfalls of your social nature. You are more in a hurry than really insensitive.

If you have a best friend, you must be careful not to put him or her on too high a pedestal, which idealistic Aries tends to do. Hurt feelings eventually result from unrealistic aims, and you can't expect anyone to be devoted exclusively to you. On the whole, however, you not only know how to please, but how to make lasting friendships. And you are loyal and openly affectionate to those you like.

ROMANCE

You are as energetic in love as in anything else. Someone to care about rounds out the rest of your life. You not only need affection; you revel in it.

Because of this, you have a tendency to fall in love with love rather than with a real person with all his faults and foibles. (Your rose-colored glasses frequently overlook these imperfections entirely until a clash occurs.)

You yearn for a lasting romance, but also have such avid curiosity that a new face intrigues you and a new fling excites you. A roving eye is all right—but only as long as no one is hurt. And what may seem to you a harmless flirtation may wound someone you have been fond of a long time.

In other words, you tend to be flighty in your romantic feelings and somewhat fickle. But when you meet someone you really care about, you change completely. Then your loyalty is steadfast and you are stubborn in your devotion and expectations. You could never say "I love you" in jest, and it would be against your nature to lead someone on. But when you get that "forever after" feeling, you are warm and demonstrative, and as possessive as you before were casual.

The Aries male makes a delightful date. He has a proud personality and great romantic appeal.

But he may be the type who takes one girl to a party and then flirts with another. Or he appears aloof and uncaring and protests that he'd "rather be with the boys." Underneath his fierce independence, the Aries male needs affection more than people from most other signs. The way to win him is not by a forceful counterattack, but by seeming as mysterious and as unflappable as possible. An open ear is another tender trap for the Aries male, who has a deep need for someone to tell his troubles to and lean on a little. Although he is a loner at times, he is deeply afraid of being lonely. He requires lots of reassurance and ego bolstering, which is never a problem because he is so dynamic and appealing.

The Aries female is equally delightful, and equally freedom-loving until someone she really cares about causes her to change her mind. (If anyone tries to make her commit herself before she is ready, she is likely to lose her temper and break up the relationship completely.)

The Aries female is caring and clever. She likes all kinds of activities and is a good sport. She doesn't mind getting her hair wet or walking to the party. She is completely feminine and charming in conversation, but also independent in what she thinks. And while she hopes to please, she would never say what she didn't believe in just to accommodate her escort.

Occasionally, the Aries female plays hard to get. This is not so much a teasing game as a real attempt to get her date to prove himself— to see if he lives up to her expectations, which are high.

In all ways the Aries female shines. But she should try to tone down her naturally competitive spirit or she might outshine her date, which no male likes, and lose in the long run.

COMPATIBILITY GUIDE

WITH ARIES: You are cut out of the same cloth, but the sparks are likely to fly—especially if you both want to take the lead. The relationship should be an active one, and can be full of zest and joy for you both—but it will require effort, and an ability to take the back seat occasionally.

WITH TAURUS: Taurus is patient and perseveres in getting what he or she wants, which may very well be you, Aires. You complement each other, and there is a strong attraction here. You are both warm-hearted and affectionate, which tempers the gap between Aries fire and Taurus practicality.

WITH GEMINI: This will be an exciting twosome. You will always be temperamentally traveling at the same pace, which is fast. You will never quite know what the other is thinking, which means that the relationship will be constantly changing. But Gemini must be careful not to provoke Aries' anger by flirting too openly.

WITH CANCER: Aries is always on the go while Cancer is content to be a homebody. And the

Aries energy and self-assurance might make moody, oversensitive Cancer feel swamped. There could be constant hurt feelings. Patience and tact will be needed if you are to find true togetherness.

WITH LEO: There should be plenty of action between you. Great vitality and a spirit of adventure add flavor to whatever you do—and that is likely to be a lot. You will probably move quickly in getting to know each other, but too much fire can burn out the relationship prematurely. Take the time to talk out small problems before they become big issues.

WITH VIRGO: Virgo equals Aries in having a keen, creative mind, but in the emotional department you are likely to clash. Aries is demonstrative; Virgo is reserved. And Virgo has a minor habit, particularly annoying to Aries, of making small criticisms and telling Aries what to do. Virgo must curb the tongue and Aries the temper for you to find mutual happiness.

WITH LIBRA: Aries is Fire and Libra is Air, which means that there are big, basic differences in the way you approach life. And Libra values contemplation whereas Aries prefers actions to words. But, as between all opposites, there is an extremely strong attraction. The two of you could easily prove the gossips wrong and achieve a stunning success together.

WITH SCORPIO: Aries may try to dominate, which makes Scorpio inwardly furious. You are intrigued by each other, but you are not likely to have a smooth time agreeing on anything. Emotions will soar and be strong. Try to be sure you are both heading in the same emotional direction.

WITH SAGITTARIUS: You both have a great flair for making friends and you will have a lot of them in common. You should make nearly ideal music together. Sagittarius brings out Aries' wit and Aries expands Sagittarius' interests and horizons. But you must avoid any struggle for power. Cooperation is the key word.

WITH CAPRICORN: Capricorn's pace is slow and steady, while Aries moves swiftly and in spurts. (Aries is likely to be the aggressor in the relationship.) You may bring out the best in each other, but it will take tolerance and understanding of quite different ways and life styles. Any break-up is likely to be sudden, and could be caused by Capricorn suspicion.

WITH AQUARIUS: You strongly attract each other and empathize deeply. And you are both very humanitarian. You are probably devoted to the same causes and have the same heroes. Any relationship is likely to be long-lasting and your dreams will doubtless come true, unless pride gets in the way. You both have wide stubborn streaks.

WITH PISCES: Pisces is shy and needs just what Aries offers: leadership and a strong shoulder to lean on. The benefits of your relationship should be mutual and richly satisfying. On the other hand, Pisces may want to attach more strings than Aries likes, which could cause Aries to suddenly bolt the scene.

TAURUS

★ *April 21 - May 20* ★

ELEMENT: *Earth*
RULED BY: *Venus*
SYMBOL: *Bull*
KEY WORD: *Warm-hearted*
JEWEL: *Jade*
COLORS: *Green, Brown, Yellow; Soft Shades*
LUCKY NUMBER: *6*
LUCKY DAY: *Friday*

OTHER IMPORTANT TAUREANS:
Albert Finney
Barbra Streisand
Sugar Ray Robinson
Margot Fonteyn
Willie Mays
Sigmund Freud
Yehudi Menuhin
Ann-Margret
Georges Braque
Bing Crosby
Salvador Dali
Queen Elizabeth II
Ella Fitzgerald
Harry S. Truman
Duke Ellington

TAURUS

GENERAL CHARACTERISTICS

OF all people, you are the most dependable. But you are by no means dull. Your approach to life is slow and steady, and your goals are most often based on traditional values. But you are also delightfully good-humored and warm-hearted. You are that unusual combination—a person who is fun and full of integrity.

Your feelings are humanitarian and your instincts kindly. You are truly "tuned in" to other people and can sense what they are thinking, often without being told. You are sympathetic and know how to communicate in the deepest sense of that word.

Though your temper is slow and you seldom fly off the handle or say anything rash, you are, on the other hand, capable of feeling anger keenly. You are furious if you think you are being taken advantage of, and you may do a slow burn for a long time after someone has thoughtlessly hurt your feelings. You are also stubborn at times. It is hard to budge you from a stand or get you to change your opinion.

Luckily, most of the time you are your easy-going self. Your wit is subtle and your smile winning, and you are far less reserved than you may seem at a first meeting. But that's your Taurean nature—to prefer the known and the comfortable. And you would far rather go to a party with a good friend than with a blind date or chance acquaintance.

You love beauty and are happiest in harmonious, lovely surroundings. But your nature is more practical than frivolous. Waste of any kind bothers you. You like ornaments that can be used and clothes that don't have to be cleaned too often. (You are also sentimental, and can't stand to throw away old blue jeans or souvenirs of good times.)

But what you keep, you keep neatly. Disorder and disarray bother you and confusion gets on your nerves. Your thinking is logical and your drawers are likely to be tidy.

And in whatever you do, you almost always have a plan. To plunge ahead slipshod is not your style. You work steadfastly and carry your ideas out to the end, long after another would have given up.

You persevere and accomplish a lot. But sometimes you are stubborn in thinking your view the only one. You would go even farther and be even better liked if you kept an open mind—and let the affectionate, fun-loving side of your nature come to the fore.

PHYSICAL CHARACTERISTICS

TAUREANS have natural good looks. Their complexions are clear (unless love of sweets leads them to overindulgence in candy and fried foods), and their hair shines with the glow of good health.

You have a great deal of energy if you are a typical Taurean, and it takes a lot to get you down physically. But when you do get that occasional flu bug or cold, you are hit harder than others. Your recuperative power is strong, but slow. And you must guard your throat especially. (Drink plenty of water and wear a muffler when it is cold.)

People born under the sign of Taurus love food and are naturally inclined to be stocky.

But you wear clothes well and like to look your best. The Taurus taste is excellent—generally striking accessories on basic, well-designed clothes. You like leisure outfits that are fun as well as comfortable, but you avoid the flamboyant and flashy. It is your aim to charm rather than startle, which you invariably do.

SCHOOL AND CAREER

TAUREANS are unusually good students, with fine work habits and strong intellectual curiosity. (You can always count on a Taurus to get his or her homework done on time.)

But the Taurus student may be a slow starter —it may take longer, initially, to grasp a new subject. But the interest, once aroused, is deep, and what is learned is almost never forgotten. Taureans have dependable memories and a mental file for facts and details that others forget.

The Taurus student is most comfortable in a routine, and in established study habits. He or she plans everything—the time, the topic, and the way an assignment is to be tackled. The Taurean mind excels at term papers but boggles a bit at surprise quizzes and class compositions.

In school, the Taurean combines tenacity with creativity. And in a career, he or she is likely to follow the same pattern.

Because Taureans love beauty, they are especially inclined toward the arts. Many are artists, decorators, and designers (anything from kitchen cabinets to cocktail dresses). Taurus influences the throat and neck, and frequently people born under this sign become singers or speakers or radio announcers. TV and politics are also favorite fields.

Cooking also fascinates Taureans, who may become dieticians or restaurant owners, or write a cookbook.

Taurean males are drawn toward the building trades: engineering, architecture, and city planning. Taurean females inspire confidence as saleswomen, beauty counselors, and teachers. And members of both sexes are outstandingly successful in the brokerage and banking businesses.

If you are a Taurus, you will work hard at whatever you do. Your way is well-disciplined, and you will stick to whatever you are doing long after another would have become discouraged and quit. This combination of control plus creativity almost always results in exceptional success, whether you choose a professional career or make a career of your home.

MONEY

TAURUS is the money sign of the Zodiac. You know how to make it and keep it, and later to manage it. Financial security frees your other creative powers. But you are never money mad. You are usually happy in your work and do such a good job that you earn more than others.

You also want more—beautiful art objects and well-made material possessions please you. Unlike many others, you are rarely taken in by the shoddy bargain or cheap article. And you will save for what you want rather than buy impulsively.

You hate waste, and would prefer to purchase something tangible than spend for pleasure—as at an expensive restaurant or popular night spot. But an occasional splurge adds spice to life and you will enjoy yourself more if you are not quite so careful.

Your tipping rarely varies and you are too inclined to divide the check exactly. On the other hand, you have strong humanitarian feelings and contribute generously to causes and school projects. What you must try to do is to be as generous in little ways as you are in the big, basic areas of life.

FUN AND LEISURE

As a Taurean, you like team sports. You are more often a supporting player than a star of the football, basketball, hockey, or swimming team. But your support is invaluable and your performance consistent.

You love the country. Picnics and walks in the woods delight you. You also like the beach, but only as long as it isn't too crowded.

Culture in almost any form is your meat. Concerts, the ballet, art and literature—all interest you though you never quite have enough time to delve as deeply as you would like.

You are moved by anything beautiful, from a sunset to a rose garden. (Gardening is a pet Taurus pastime.) You also delight in good food, both eating and preparing it. Of all the signs, you are the most appreciative person to have over for dinner.

And you love to have people over. Entertaining is another favorite hobby. In some areas of your life you are rather rigid, but as a host or hostess you are relaxed, and delightful fun.

Other people and places interest you, but you get actively homesick when you are away for too long a time. You prefer a familiar place that is not too far, and weekends to long trips. And you would always rather go with family or friends rather than be with strangers.

HOME AND FAMILY

You are a real homebody. You enjoy your family and "just hanging around the house."

You like order and harmonious surroundings. Your closets are likely to be tidy and you feel most comfortable when you know just where everything is. It bothers you terribly if you have to share a room with a brother or sister who is messy.

You have an excellent eye for color, and like beauty as well as comfort. Any advice you give on decorating is well worth listening to. And while you lean toward the traditional, the total look you like is never outdated.

Because you also love beautiful scenery, you have a special yen for the country. And if you can't be there, you will do the next best thing— arrange flowers or grow plants or put up scenic posters.

Wherever you are, you like to have people visit you. The welcome mat is always out, and you entertain casually and well. You have that knack for making others feel just as at home as you do.

In your relationships with your parents, you are self-reliant and self-controlled. You rarely clash, but you do fret, and sometimes aren't quite so sure of yourself as you seem. Even the smallest criticism cuts, while praise and admiration make you blossom and do your best. Attention and encouragement are what you need, for you are a far finer person than you sometimes think.

FRIENDSHIP

PEOPLE seek you out as a friend. You are warm-hearted and easygoing, and you make others feel relaxed and happy. You want the best for your friends. You also are aware of the little things that please, and rarely forget a birthday or a friend's favorite color.

You are gentle and kind, and slow to anger. But this doesn't mean that you never get mad. It takes a lot and a long time for you to lose your temper, but when you do, your fury can be almost frightening. Your friends should know you well enough to realize that it is a case of the straw that broke the camel's back. When things go wrong, anger builds up because you find it hard to release your feelings in little ways.

But you can laugh at yourself, and though you take life and your friends seriously, you enjoy jokes and gentle teasing.

You are a good listener, full of sympathy and understanding. And any advice you give is tempered with tact and meant to be constructive.

It may take you a while to get to know a person, but the friendships you form are usually lasting. You never "drop" people or let sudden whims and enthusiasms shake the foundations of your friendships.

ROMANCE

You naturally attract romance. You are affectionate and your emotions are deep. Yours is a quiet charm, not the kind that bowls the other person over—the kind that draws a person to you with a slow and steady pull. "I can't get her out of my mind," or "I miss so-and-so more than I thought" are frequently said about you.

The love you need is steadfast and warm, and you are most capable of returning these qualities. You are not impulsive. You rarely fall in love at first sight and it takes you a while to open up your whole personality to another person.

Physical and mental attraction are both important to you. You want to have a lot in common, to be able to like the same sports and laugh at the same jokes. Sharing and giving are strong in your make-up. And you could never really care for anyone who didn't think your ideas and values were important too. (On the other hand, you may not be entirely flexible about trying to see his or her point of view if it is different from yours.)

It is not in your nature to lose your head or do anything rash, but you are an emotional person and you feel strongly possessive about the object of your affection. You will be deeply hurt if he or she flirts openly or takes you lightly in any way. When you give your heart, it is in earnest, and for a long time.

The Taurus male is dependable and stead-fast, and a delightful companion. He is also unusually attractive in a strong, silent way, and has a surprising, underlying sense of humor.

But he is cautious, and he is a little hard to get. He expects a real person behind a pretty face and is rarely misled by glamour or surface charm.

Because of this, he often has a number of companionable attachments before he finds someone to whom he really feels close. When he finally makes up his mind romantically, he usually makes a wise choice, and the relation-ship is likely to be exceptionally happy.

The Taurus female is sincere and a little naive. She believes in love and in the goodness of people. She is so romantic and idealistic that she occasionally falls in love with someone who is merely leading her on.

But her sound instincts and sense of propor-tion save her from making any serious mis-takes. And she is slow to make any commit-ment.

Most often she has many admirers, though she is not a flirt and she is never a tease. Her affections are quiet—but only until they are really aroused. For once the Taurus female falls in love, she is openly joyous and responsive, and is likely to form an attachment that may even be the love of her life.

COMPATIBILITY GUIDE

WITH ARIES: You are both fun-loving and have many friends. Taurus' calm temperament soothes fiery Aries, while Aries brings out Taurus' warmth and enthusiasm. There may be minor irritations based on differences in pace (Taurus slow-moving; Aries impulsive), but the relationship should end successfully.

WITH TAURUS: The two of you may have pleasant times, but there probably isn't quite enough excitement to keep you interested in each other exclusively. You may tend to take each other for granted. It could take a third person to spark you into action, for your natures are both possessive, and you will fight stubbornly when aroused.

WITH GEMINI: Gemini might easily be too restless for stable, stay-at-home Taurus. On the other hand, Gemini excites Taurus and brings out untapped depths of affection. The combination of the capricious and the practical could be the beginning of a lasting and lively relationship.

WITH CANCER: Taurus' even and pleasant temper should help Cancer stabilize occasional bouts of moodiness. You are naturally sympathetic toward each other and there is a strong magnetic pull. Together you should find much joy. And a once-in-a-while quarrel only makes making-up that much better.

WITH LEO: The possibilities are promising as long as you keep the lines of communication open. Stubborn silence on Taurus' part could make Leo lose control and leave. But both of you will probably make the effort it takes because your very differences are what you find fascinating in each other.

WITH VIRGO: You have the same ideals and the same approach to problems. You are both sincere and compatible. But if you care, don't keep it a secret. Virgo can be reserved or warmly affectionate—and it is likely that Taurus will have to make the first move. This is a twosome that may bloom beautifully but slowly.

WITH LIBRA: Libra lives for today while Taurus is a planner. Also, Libra is spendthrift while Taurus would rather save for that rainy day.

Luckily, Libra has the charm and diplomacy to adjust, and Taurus has the patience to work toward a goal. You might make it—and swimmingly.

WITH SCORPIO: Taurus, who likes everything laid out on the table, may have trouble understanding Scorpio, who is secretive and complicated and tends to cover up deep feelings. Affection and patient understanding are the keys to communication between the two of you. After you get over the hurdles, you should be very happy.

WITH SAGITTARIUS: High-spirited, impulsive Sagittarius may rock Taurus' steady boat. And Taurus may want to relax and spend a lazy day just when social Sagittarius yearns to find some action. Your basic life styles are very different, but you are bound to stimulate and excite each other, which could lead to a happy ending.

WITH CAPRICORN: You both like the same things and look toward the future. You will appreciate each other and probably have few problems concerning plans and joint friends. Spice may be the missing ingredient in your relationship. A few more laughs *now* may be just what you need.

WITH AQUARIUS: Aquarius' desire for freedom and change may baffle Taurus. And Aquarius may counterattack with the claim that Taurus is a stick-in-the-mud and takes life far too seriously. Fortunately, you both can laugh at yourselves and both have the capacity to adjust. Success depends on how much you want to.

WITH PISCES: You have secretly yearned for each other all along. Taurus yens for the intensity and sympathy Pisces gives, and Pisces yens for the deep-rooted security and self-confidence that are so much a part of the Taurus make-up. Occasional snags and hurt feelings shouldn't mar the depths of your togetherness.

GEMINI

★ *May 21 - June 20* ★

ELEMENT: *Air*
RULED BY: *Mercury*
SYMBOL: *Twins*
KEY WORD: *Changeable*
JEWEL: *Alexandrite*
COLORS: *Violet, Green, Blue, Gold;*
Irridescent Shades
LUCKY NUMBER: *5*
LUCKY DAY: *Wednesday*

OTHER IMPORTANT GEMINIANS:
Bob Dylan
Ian Fleming
Marilyn Monroe
Jean-Paul Sartre
Burl Ives
Paul Gauguin
Judy Garland
Dean Martin
Laurence Olivier
John Wayne
Peggy Lee
John F. Kennedy
Bob Hope
Igor Stravinsky

GEMINI

GEMINI is the sign of duality. Like the Twins, your symbol, you have two distinct natures. You have an agile, bright mind and a gay, fun-loving personality. You are both detached and deeply dependent on affection. You are sociable and somewhat of a loner.

You might say that change is the most constant aspect of your being. You are serious and silly, opinionated and broadminded, ambitious and timid, happy and moody—all by turns. No one is ever quite sure what you are going to say or do next—sometimes you are not quite sure yourself.

Moreover, your enthusiasms are constantly changing. They are strong, but likely to be short lived—whether they are for a friend, a food, or a new fashion. You become very "hot" on someone or something and then suddenly lose interest. Your inconstancy is charming, but others find you hard to pin down. They wonder

48

if your whim of the moment is what you really want.

Certainly you are always on the lookout for fresh ideas and new adventures. You have an avid curiosity and want to know everything about everything there is. The only trouble is that you are likely to have so many irons in the fire you find it hard to follow through and finish any one project. You have many talents, but you are in danger of becoming a dabbler unless you learn to organize your time and finish what you start. You are likely to take a few art lessons and then switch to music, or start making a dress and drop it midway because you have a sudden urge to write poetry. By spreading the field too far, you dilute your efforts and have less to show than you should.

But, for all your changeability and charm, you are also a very logical person. You can follow facts through to their conclusion. And when a really important decision is to be made, you are more likely to be guided by logic and common sense than by your emotions.

Your surface nature is volatile, with feelings like quicksilver and moods that are always going up or down. But underneath you are reasonable, and you "keep your cool" in almost any situation. More than others, your opinion is unbiased because you can see both sides of any question. You are also surprisingly accurate and farsighted in your thinking. And your basic attitude toward life is optimistic.

You like a lot of color and excitement, and have the ability to turn whatever you do into a real happening. Dull routine bores you and you could never be called a plodder. You prefer to act on impulse. Mentally and physically, you are likely to be here one minute, then "gone with the wind," which is natural because yours is an Air sign. And wherever you go, you bring wit, and the special, effervescent charm characteristic of Gemini.

PHYSICAL CHARACTERISTICS

YOUR body is as active as your mind. Your energy is boundless and you keep on the go longer than others. You are frequently asked, "Don't you ever get tired?" You say "no," but this isn't entirely realistic. You are inclined to live on your nerves to too great an extent and eventually suffer from fatigue and exhaustion.

And when you are tired, you are more susceptible to colds and other illnesses. Luckily, your constitution is basically strong, so you recuperate quickly. But to prevent problems, be sure to get enough rest. Eat well and relax once in a while.

Geminians generally have small bones and fine features. Females born under the sign have a delicate look and are very feminine. Gemini males are exceptionally handsome and have animated, interesting faces. Both move gracefully and have unusually good coordination. And both have eyes that are expressive and sometimes seem to change color.

Blue, violet, white, and gold are favorite Gemini colors. Geminians of both sexes like clothes—different types and frequent changes of costume. You never know what a Gemini is going to wear next.

The Gemini female is fascinated by anything new. But she particularly loves dresses that are flowing and made of somewhat filmy materials. On the other hand, she has a weakness for long hair and old-fashioned jewelry.

The Gemini male enjoys looking a bit different. His preference is for the bright and slightly sporty. And he always looks like the individualist he is.

SCHOOL AND CAREER

YOUR mind is quick and agile. As a Gemini, you should do well in school—except that you may have difficulty concentrating on one thing at a time. You are naturally inquisitive, but you are better at starting than finishing projects and assignments. Anything that takes long, continued effort, like a lengthy term paper, is alien to your nature. You prefer to tackle several short assignments at once, skipping from one to the other until you are finished. In other words, you thrive on variety, and your creative energy is released by stimulation rather than by an intense focus on one type of work.

Though you are talented and fond of learning, at times you tend to "just skim by." You may waste time and try to substitute cleverness for continuous hard work. This is a shame, because you are capable of making top grades.

Later, your career should be one which makes use of your many leanings and talents. Most likely you will prefer to be your own boss or be the creative head of a group. (You are not only creative yourself but are a natural expert at picking the brains of others to best advantage.)

You are an excellent speaker and can write and talk fluently and clearly. Therefore, you are naturally suited to radio and television work, or to be a politician or company spokesman. Since you express yourself so well, you might want to be a critic, journalist, or art director in advertising.

And because Geminians of both sexes speak

with conviction as well as good humor, you might pick a selling job—anything from cars to cosmetics. You also know a good bargain, and can correctly size up your prospective client.

Gemini males are exceptionally dexterous and are especially suited to be surgeons, dentists, and mechanics. And because their minds are impartial, they are excellent at anything that requires counseling or creative troubleshooting.

Gemini females are frequently top models and actresses because they can literally take on any face. They also make the best "girl Fridays" of any of the signs. And when an executive says he couldn't do without his secretary, she is most likely to be a Gemini.

MONEY

You like to do things and have things—and money is one of them. You are not stingy or materialistic, but you do thoroughly enjoy life and the monetary rewards of a job well done. You like to travel, to entertain, and to be well dressed—and all these things require cash.

You are not, however, naturally good at steady saving. You would rather spend now, and not think about tomorrow. Therefore, you occasionally fall for bargains you don't need and spur-of-the-moment purchases you can't really afford. If you always stopped to think before you said "yes," you would be in a better position financially. And though you hate the word budget, you of all people could benefit from one.

But while you are not naturally economical and rarely plan, you do have good basic money sense. You are adept at finding ways of supplementing your allowance and creating a demand for your services, from baby-sitting to car washing. Haste is your only serious financial problem. Take a good long look at anything before you get involved, even if it's lending more than you should to a good friend. Otherwise, you are generous, capable, and creative where money is concerned.

FUN AND LEISURE

As a Gemini, you hate to sit still. You are perpetually alert and active. You are not a natural spectator but prefer sports in which you participate. In summer you delight in swimming, sailing, tennis, and ping pong, while in winter you have an equal zest for skiing, skating, sledding, and anything new, such as snowmobiling.

You love the theater—slightly preferring live performances to the movies. You also enjoy concerts and art shows. You like to take part yourself, and may belong to a little theater group or be a Saturday painter.

In music your tastes are as dual as everything else about you. The intellectual side of you leans toward Bach, Brahms, and Beethoven, while the social, active side of your nature thrives on Johnny Cash and the Supremes. In books, you like anything that is short, wittily written, and handy. You are much more likely to pick up the latest magazine than read a long, leisurely novel.

All social occasions, even unexpected guests, make you happy. And you are one of the few types who really enjoys guessing games and costume parties. You, in fact, prefer an evening with an element of surprise rather than a too planned party. You are quick and bright at repartee and, if an evening is dull, are likely to liven it up yourself by your own wit and personality.

Gemini is an Air sign, and anywhere the wind blows is where you like to go. You actually *need* a change of scene from time to time if you are to be happy at home and in your daily routine.

When you travel, you are responsive and eager. You fit in with any type of person, any place. You are so absorbed you are likely to come back with a slightly different accent and a suitcase full of souvenirs. Finally, what others might think of as a frantic, fast-paced trip is, to you, a rest.

HOME AND FAMILY

IN spite of your sometimes flighty ways, you are a surprisingly strong family person. Your sense of home and parents may be so strong because you are away and on the go more than others. And more than others, you need a home base to return to, and the security of loving and knowing you are loved.

But even your home is not likely to be quiet with you in it. You enjoy having people over. The welcome mat is always out and you are never annoyed at being interrupted. Friends may drop in and brothers and sisters may knock on your door at any time.

Your own room is likely to be a center of activity, with sports equipment and trappings from your many hobbies. Bookshelves will be brimming and tabletops filled with evidences of your many interests. Colors are likely to be bright, and the atmosphere comfortable and inviting.

For the most part, your relationship with your parents should be relaxed and good. But occasionally the duality of your Gemini nature comes to the fore. Then your family may find you somewhat hard to understand and handle. Because your nature is plastic, you see so many sides to a given question that you end up confusing yourself. Then you may resent advice when your parents try to give it. It is important to remember that they love you and are only trying to help you sort things—and your own feelings—out. Your oversensitivity to what you think is criticism only further reflects your inner doubts.

Fortunately, most of the time your attitude is positive and your feelings are openly affectionate. And when you feel depressed or at cross purposes with yourself and others, it never lasts long. That's because you get up and act, rather than wallow in problems. Your basic attitude is ever optimistic and on the bright side.

FRIENDSHIP

A GEMINI loves to explore—mountains and unmarked paths, and, most of all, new people. As a Gemini, you genuinely enjoy meeting strangers and making new friends. You are outgoing, and are not in the least thrown by groups where you don't know anyone or by going places alone. That's because you usually aren't alone for long. You make small talk with ease and are never shy about introducing yourself.

Certainly it is difficult to picture you alone for any length of time. You like to have plenty of activity, and plenty of people around. You want to be where the action is, and that always includes others.

Moreover, you are frank and fair with friends. And you expect them to be honest and open in return. You try hard never to say anything that isn't so, and you find it hard to forgive a friend who misleads you in any way. When this happens, you are likely to flash back with a sharp comment or cutting remark. For, in spite of your seemingly easygoing appearance, you are deeply sensitive to slights.

But you are a good and loyal friend. You are generous and sympathetic and try never to let a friend down. On the negative side, you sometimes get involved with too many people at once, and other times your friends find you a little hard to figure out. You say one thing today and another tomorrow.

If they are good friends, they will realize that you mean both things sincerely—at the time. It's just that change is the essence of you as a Gemini.

But while your opinions change frequently and you are somewhat fickle about chance acquaintances, your loyalties are deep and lasting where close friends are concerned. Your caring is constant and you are likely to keep them for life.

ROMANCE

You like as much variety in love as you do in anything else. Therefore, you are frequently accused of being fickle.

This is not entirely true, for you are totally committed—while you are committed—to a particular person. It's just that you change your mind frequently. When ties get too binding, you get nervous and are likely to look for a new romance. You may even break off the old relationship completely.

On the other hand, you are capable of deep and lasting feeling. Your nature is basically affectionate. Your desire for constant change, a new face or a new relationship, lasts only until you have met the one who arouses your deep and most sincere interest. Then you become as steadfast and as sure of your feelings as you before were flighty and wavering. Then, too, you stop looking around, and are actually more content than others to be a one-person person.

But until you find a truly meaningful relationship, you love to flirt. And you do it in a gay, delightful way. You never deceive, and could never say "I love you" unless you really meant it. But you do enjoy being thoroughly feminine or masculine, and your date is likely to get the impression that you are serious simply because you are so charming.

You never lie romantically or lead others on, but you do hurt people unwittingly. Sometimes you do this by telling too much of the truth—for instance, that your feelings have changed and you would rather not see so much of a certain person. Honesty is a part of your nature, but you should try to temper it with more tact.

Because you like variety in romance, you may marry later than people from other signs. A long period of exploration and testing is important to you. It would be a mistake to tie yourself down before you are absolutely sure that "this is *it*."

The Gemini male may be hard to catch. He likes to play the field. He has many dates with different types and a "don't fence me in" attitude.

If you are interested in a Gemini male, the best way to win him is by seeming casual about the relationship yourself. And you must definitely let him take the lead. He has a delightful, dry wit and he is a stimulating companion, but he will be off with the wind if he senses he is being pursued.

The Gemini female is an exciting type. She literally sparkles, and seems interested in everything her date says. Her absorption is total even if it is not always permanent.

The Gemini female loves surprises and to "do something different." She is delighted by small personal gifts and thoughtful gestures, like a friend remembering to call her when she has a cold.

Her sense of freedom is strong and she is slightly stubborn about giving it up—and no one can convince her by a direct attack. She commits herself romantically only when she is fully convinced, and the person who does not push her is most likely to succeed.

COMPATIBILITY GUIDE

WITH ARIES: This has every chance of being an exceptionally successful relationship. Aries provides Gemini with plenty of variety and stimulation—and Aries, being a born leader, knows how to talk Gemini out of occasional moodiness. Gemini spices the twosome with wit and warmth. You both give each other plenty of freedom, which can bring about the closest bond.

WITH TAURUS: This combination works as long as you don't try to change each other. Taurus may seem too sober for flighty Gemini, and Gemini may seem impossibly indecisive to plan-ahead Taurus. Actually, you are good for each other, but it will take effort to find this out.

WITH GEMINI: You should either drive each other mad or have a delightful relationship. Too much flirting and too many outside interests could be negative influences. But, on the positive side, there is strong mutual attraction and you have many hobbies in common.

WITH CANCER: Super-sensitive Cancer may have constantly hurt feelings in this combination. Also, Cancer prefers a more quiet way of life, whereas Gemini is always running around looking for "something new." The possibilities are positive only if you are emotional about the same things. It will be important to keep the lines of communication open.

WITH LEO: Two on-the-go people with great capacities for fun should make a delightful team. You are likely to go far together and have a lot of happy times. Strong, loving Leo is the perfect type to curb Gemini restlessness. And Gemini loves to look up to someone strong, someone who is as decisive as Gemini is uncertain.

WITH VIRGO: Virgo is likely to be too practical for unconventional Gemini. And Gemini's liking for the odd and offbeat might irritate Virgo to the point of a real breakup. You are not naturally compatible with each other, and would really have to want to make things work out if you are to find mutual happiness. That is possible but not probable.

WITH LIBRA: This way, that way Gemini needs a strong, steady partner to give her a sense of direction. Libra should be just the one! And the charming Libra personality is more than capable of holding Gemini's interest. Both of you are affectionate and you also have a lot in common intellectually. Moreover, you are both Air signs, which means that you like to be on the go together.

WITH SCORPIO: The magnetic attraction is likely to be strong. But you really have little in common, and Gemini's flirtatious nature is likely to make Scorpio furious. Suspicion could wreck your relationship. Happiness between you is possible only if you both are adaptable, and can quarrel constructively rather than dig at each other.

WITH SAGITTARIUS: Two bright people with strongly gregarious natures should hit it off well. And you usually do. But the relationship may be more a friendship than anything serious. Or, you might date and break up and then eventually get together on a more lasting basis. The possibilities for something permanent are strong.

WITH CAPRICORN: Capricorn is likely to find Gemini irresponsible, and may even disapprove of non-conformist Gemini. Capricorn will have to let up a little if there is to be any lasting relationship. Moreover, Capricorn is a planner while Gemini lives life in the present and to the hilt. Both of you would have to work hard to see the other's viewpoint.

WITH AQUARIUS: Intellectually you are ideal companions. You both have outside interests in common and provide each other with the stimulation and excitement you both need. And because you let each other do his or her thing, your relationship is likely to be closer and longer than if you acted possessively.

WITH PISCES: Insecure Pisces may want so many reassurances that Gemini really cares, that Gemini may start feeling the relationship is somewhat of a drag. On the other hand, dependent Pisces may be just the emotional anchor will-o'-the-wisp Gemini needs. Your wave lengths are different, but happiness is possible if you keep tuned in to each other's feelings as well as words.

CANCER

★ *June 21 - July 20* ★

ELEMENT: *Water*
RULED BY: *Moon*
SYMBOL: *Crab*
KEY WORD: *Impressionable*
JEWEL: *Aquamarine*
COLORS: *White, Yellow, Blue;*
Luminescent Shades
LUCKY NUMBER: *2*
LUCKY DAY: *Saturday*

OTHER IMPORTANT CANCERIANS:
Ringo Starr
John Glenn
Andrew Wyeth
Polly Bergen
David Brinkley
Van Cliburn
Phyllis Diller
Lena Horne
Gian-Carlo Menotti
Nelson Rockefeller
Duke of Windsor
Louis Armstrong
Marc Chagall
Helen Keller

CANCER

To you, feeling is all important. And you are emotional even in your thinking. Certainly you are one of the most sensitive of all the signs.

Your personality is generally warm and you are sympathetic toward others. But, though you are basically affectionate, you are sometimes too shy to show your feelings. Your kindness is instinctive because you can always put yourself in another person's place.

Your empathy is a fine thing, although from time to time you get so involved in how other people feel that you lose sight of your own feelings. In other words, you are so impressionable that you tend to take on the moods, personal traits, and opinions of your associates. If they are in high spirits, you are equally excited. And if they are feeling depressed, your mood is equally low. You are not so much weak as extra-sensitive, so that a stronger, more aggressive personality can make you act not at all like yourself. You should realize your susceptibility and practice being your real Cancerian self, which is warm-hearted and thoroughly delightful. You also have an almost extra-sensory kind of intuition that is unique.

Because you are an emotional person, you tend to dramatize small things. It is hard for you to say no—to refuse a date you're not really interested in or a request for help. (And sometimes you later resent being taken advantage of.) Also, criticism of any kind can make you climb into your shell. For underneath your apparently shy nature, you long for admiration, and need and want a pat on the back more than others. What you most lack is a strong sense of self-confidence. This can be developed, but it takes time and patience. Also, sometimes you are too hard on yourself.

From time to time you feel sorry for yourself. You may exaggerate small slights—or imagine them entirely, as when a friend has been curt because he's in a hurry rather than because he's angry at you. When this happens, you are inclined to brood instead of act. You worry more than you should, although really bad things rarely happen to you. It is wonderful that you have such a lively imagination, but for you it is important that you use is for positive purposes. Fear, not fact, is your sometimes enemy.

Of all the signs you are the most mystic. Your

intuition is keen and you have a deep sense of religion. You also have an excellent memory and a vivid sense of the past. Music, religion, and the arts interest you, as do all things occult and mysterious which cannot be scientifically proved—like astrology.

Though your nature is quiet, you are definitely not a loner. You very much need someone to confide in and care about, and you would always rather go somewhere with someone.

Praise and confidence are what double your energies. You are never really lazy, but can give this appearance when paralyzed by self-doubt. It is curious that your intuition, so strong in other ways, never fully convinces you of your own worth—which is great indeed.

PHYSICAL CHARACTERISTICS

MOODS affect your health, which is basically good. Even a common cold can set you imagining all sorts of dire things, and you sometimes take on the worries of others to too great an extent.

When this happens, your stomach is most likely to be affected, for, physically, that is your weak point. Also, more than others, you are likely to turn to food when you are feeling a little depressed. This is all right if you are the tall, slender type of Cancerian. However, many members of your sign have weight problems. And while the strict discipline of a diet is unnatural to you, it is best to catch those few extra pounds at the start.

All Cancerians are generally small-boned and well-proportioned. Cancer females have rather dreamy, sometimes ethereal, expressions. Cancer males appear to be mild-mannered but have a great deal of get-up-and-go when motivated.

Both Cancer males and females love clothes, and are particularly intrigued by clothes that relate to the past or to other countries, or which have mystic overtones. Cancer females love long dresses—anything flowing and romantic and feminine. And the fabrics are likely to be more poetic than practical. Silk and dotted swiss are favorites.

Color preferences for both sexes are blue, pale green, and yellow. Above all, white is the special favorite.

SCHOOL AND CAREER

You have an excellent memory, and are able to understand the present by studying the past. In school, you are likely to excel in history, languages, and social studies. Also, you are able to mesh different kinds of knowledge and are deeply aware of how today's changing standards reflect past events and ideas.

You are a good, and generally careful, student. However, at times you daydream rather than do. Other times you sit back and remain silent in class when you should speak out. Timidity may cause this. Or you may be afraid of being laughed at or criticized. Most of the time you have the right answer, and certainly you are one of the most imaginative of any of the signs. By getting involved you will make the most of your fine scholastic talents.

When you choose a career, you quite likely will be drawn to one with a humanitarian theme. Cancer males make outstanding doctors and psychiatrists, and Cancer females are among the best nurses. You may also do social work. And peace drives and poverty programs concern you more than others.

Whatever you do, you have a strong sense of duty and are loyal to your employer. You are creative, and often accomplish in a quiet way twice as much as others who brag and boast while you work away at a given task.

As a Cancerian you are artistic, and also have a more than average love of food, so that you might be a dietician or own a restaurant (which would be noted for its atmosphere as well as food). You are also fascinated by anything concerned with the sea. Commerce, shipping, and travel all interest you.

Your curiosity and creative sense should make you invaluable in advertising. You might even work in your home, as yours is the home sign of the Zodiac. Cancer females are especially likely to design or do something creative on a free-lance basis. But whatever you create —toys, clothes, or a better mousetrap—you must learn to take some risks and not care so much what people say about you. Success always attracts some jealousy, and with your talents and temperament, you are more than likely to lead whatever field you choose.

MONEY

MONEY does not mean a great deal to you. You like to be comfortable, but your tastes are basically modest. Spending for show bothers you, and you are generous but never extravagant just to impress. For instance, you would never give a flamboyant or embarrassingly expensive gift. But you are giving and thoughtful in little ways.

Also, you are sentimental, even about things

which cost money. You love a particular tie or piece of jewelry because a particular someone has given it to you. And you buy because an article suits your mood, not because it is a better bargain.

Financial integrity comes naturally to you, and you have an excellent sense of values. You have a flair for making money and the farsightedness to put some aside "just in case." You put little store by material things, but you worry unless you have some security. You are not a gambler, yet oddly you are lucky. And while you are never quite sure of yourself or of the future, you almost always do well monetarily.

FUN AND LEISURE

CANCERIANS are drawn to quieter pastimes than some other signs. For instance, you are more likely to swim than play soccer, to sail than toboggan. In sports you are drawn to the seashore, just as the moon, your influencing celestial body, is pulled by the tides.

You also enjoy watching sports that demand agility as well as strength. You are an enthusiastic fan, and are completely emotional about your favorite team.

Nature and her moods mean a great deal to

you, too. You love to walk, especially on a moonlit night. The first snow and the first spring flower delight you equally.

You respond intuitively to games such as poker, bridge, and checkers. You play well—not according to facts and averages, but according to your "feel" about a given hand. Others say you are lucky.

You are happiest at home and are almost certain to have some sort of collection, which is likely to have something to do with history. You also spend a great deal of your time reading and listening to music. In both you respond to an aura of mystery and romance. You like to entertain, preferably very small groups at your own home. Loud, noisy parties frighten you a little. You tend to feel swamped and "out of it." But you shine in your own surroundings. Even soul-searching with one close friend is to you a delightful and fulfilling evening,

In travel, your preference is for scenery and historic sites. And the visual and emotional impact of a place or people mean more to you than the bare facts. You are one of the most creative travelers. You can find poetry in even a bare city building.

You always fit in with others rather than try to impose your own ideas—and because of this, you are a welcomed guest, though you may not want to be away from home as often as others.

HOME AND FAMILY

No one is happier at home or closer to his family than you are. You are so devoted that, at times, you may be too dependent on what they say. Many signs rebel and try to break away as soon as possible, but not you. You prefer to have someone to lean on, and the outside world sometimes frightens you. Moreover, you prefer the familiar: your room, your chair, your things in the places where you put them.

In your own surroundings, you are most sure of yourself. Cancer females love to cook, garden, and decorate, and Cancer males often have a workshop, or at least one collection. And both are likely to prefer antique to modern furniture.

As a Cancerian, you are not only most comfortable in your home, but you are loyal to other family members. You are cheerful when asked to help around the house and are considerate of any brothers and sisters.

The only problems occur when your oversensitivity makes you feel injured, as when someone has spoken to you hastily or impulsively. An ill-chosen word can send you into your shell of reserve, and it is important for you to realize that much of what is said in any home is casual. Also, when you are bothered, it is better to talk out the problem than to brood about it. However, because you are so sensitive and creative, you will probably figure this out for yourself. Your natural intuition is usually wise and your imagination is unfettered, in spite of your opposite need to be sheltered and protected.

FRIENDSHIP

You have many friends because you are essentially sympathetic and receptive. However, many times your friends set the tone of the relationship. You are so impressionable that if they are strong types or Fire signs (Aries, Leo, and Sagittarius), you are likely to take on their colors rather than be totally yourself.

When this happens, you falter in taking definite action and let the other person chart the course of your relationship. Underneath, you are dying for your own place in the sun, and to be not only appreciated but applauded. The main problem is communication. You are exceptionally sensitive, but sometimes have trouble saying how you feel in just so many words. When you finally learn to speak up, your relationships will be smoother. And most likely the moodiness, so much a part of the Cancer temperament, will be lessened. For once anything is out in the air it loses its sting.

You may be intimidated by strong-minded friends. But you love to talk things over with soul mates who are equally imaginative and emotional. Just be sure you listen as well as tell, which shouldn't be any problem because your empathy is strong.

Moreover, you are a kind, generous friend. You never forget a kindness and you are always willing to go more than halfway in your relationships with others.

You have many acquaintances, but your intimate friends are likely to be close and few, and you often idealize and romanticize them. If for any reason you lose a good friend, you are shattered, and naturally assume it is your fault —which is typical of your tendency to take too much of the blame. You will be happier when you learn to like yourself as well as others like you.

ROMANCE

It would be hard to imagine you without some romantic attachment, for you are affectionate, loyal, and intensely emotional. You are extremely susceptible to the opposite sex, and you are thoroughly sentimental rather than sensible in your approach to love.

Sometimes you give the impression of being fickle, that your feelings are based more on the whim of the moment than on any firm foundation. Other times, you are terribly interested in a person, get to know that person better, and then, suddenly, become strange and standoffish. The latter usually happens because you don't know how to get out of a relationship once you sense it isn't for you. You hate to hurt others as much as you hate to be hurt. You end up by acting difficult and defensive when you are really feeling trapped. Even if you wound another person momentarily, it is always better to try to talk things out.

Your standards are high and you expect a lot in love. You are extremely sympathetic, and expect the same kind of intense response to your troubles that you give to the other person's. You expect the kind of bond "beyond words."

Such a relationship is hard to find, so you may date many before you find "the" one. But when you are serious, there is no question about it. When you are deeply committed, you have no desire to flirt or play around. And you are extremely possessive in your own quiet way. Also, though you deal with real problems very well, you are likely to imagine slights in love, sometimes where none were intended.

The Cancer male is intense and romantic. He has a fascination all his own. He is hard to get, but his attachment, once made, is likely to be lasting.

He is a delightful date who makes a real effort to tune in on his companion's wave length. In case of a quarrel, he may become moody or show a stubborn streak, but only until he is reassured of the affection he craves.

The Cancer female loves to be protected. She makes any date feel more masculine, though occasionally she goes too far in "testing" affection. Then she becomes over-possessive and demanding, and may be emotional over the most minor matter—like which movie to go to.

Happily, most of the time she is her affectionate self and will go to any length to please the person she is with. She knows her feminine role and loves it—and so quite easily finds love in return.

COMPATIBILITY GUIDE

WITH ARIES: Both of you are basically affectionate, but you may not understand each other's way of expressing emotion. Aries may come on too strong for shy, sensitive Cancer. Also, the Aries temperament is forthright and the Aries life style is to be always on the go.

Cancer is reserved and a natural homebody. The relationship has the best chance of success if Aries uses his or her natural talent for leadership to "bring out" Cancer.

WITH TAURUS: Practical Taurus is a good, stabilizing influence on moody, insecure Cancer. You are not alike, but you complement each other's needs. And because you are both caring types, the relationship should be a happy one. And Taurus should benefit greatly from Cancer's imaginative touch.

WITH GEMINI: The two of you are likely to wallow constantly in hurt feelings. The trouble is that flighty Gemini can make Cancer feel even less sure of him- or herself. Geminians must watch what is said, even in jest. And Cancerians must learn to laugh at themselves. Taking things less seriously will make the possibilities far more positive.

WITH CANCER: Two such finely tuned sensibilities could clash. You both have the same weaknesses, and the same things are likely to irritate you. But you are attracted to each other, and the very intensity of your feeling could lead to a lasting rapport. Emotional control and maturity will be needed to make this relationship a success.

WITH LEO: Leo will probably want to dominate Cancer, which is fine as long as more forceful Leo does not take advantage of the role. Also, Cancer must learn to bring hurt feelings out into the open. Communication can prevent many problems, and it would be a shame if pride destroyed this otherwise excellent twosome. Cancer yearns to be taken care of, and no one is more capable of it than a Leo.

WITH VIRGO: You are well suited to each other. You are both affectionate and level-headed, and you both enjoy harmonious living and yen for security. The relationship should be responsive, with Virgo acting as a steadying influence on Cancer, and Cancer adding fire to Virgo's somewhat less imaginative approach to life.

WITH LIBRA: Your natures are not basically compatible, and you may get on each other's nerves. Libra is far more extravagant and loves to be out on the town. And Libra is ruled by the mind, whereas Cancer is an almost totally emotional person. Libra must make an extra effort to be considerate and affectionate in little ways if the two of you are to make it together.

WITH SCORPIO: You are well suited—in both mind and feeling. You bring out the best in each other and understand what less sensitive signs would never see in the other person. Scorpio gives shy, sometimes withdrawn Cancer someone to relate to meaningfully. And Cancer's common sense is badly needed by ~orpio. You both need plenty of emotional attraction which shouldn't be any problem since ~~tr~~action is so strong.

WITH SAGITTA~~R~~. Sagittarius may make ~~a~~ trouble here is that rather than protected. Also, ~~Sagit~~tarian restlessness may make Cancer even le~~ss~~ secure. And though you both have a sense of hum~~or~~, you may not laugh at the same things. Effort, and constant caring, will be needed to make the relationship fulfilling rather than frustrating.

WITH CAPRICORN: Insecure Cancer can benefit from Capricorn's self-confidence. On the other hand, Capricorn should curb a tendency to be too frank and, at times, too faultfinding. The danger here is not of a clash, but rather of Cancer withdrawing. On the plus side, you both have strong feelings about love and loyalty, and just could bring off a stunning success.

WITH AQUARIUS: Aquarius is easy for Cancer to get along with, but may not be emotionally satisfying. Cancer is an inner-directed person, whereas Aquarius is sometimes more concerned with brotherhood than personal love. And Aquarius is far more independent. However, if the Aquarian is of the affectionate type and emotionally mature, he or she should mak high-strung Cancer an ideal match.

WITH PISCES: Both of you appr should feel out the best in each oth thoughtfulness secure and happy the genuine match-mates. and sensitivity fully to each other that even You respond (and inevitable) hurt feelings occasional shouldn't last long.

LEO

★ *July 21 - August 21* ★

ELEMENT: *Fire*
RULED BY: *Sun*
SYMBOL: *Lion*
KEY WORD: *Loving*
JEWEL: *Ruby*
COLORS: *Fire-Red, Orange, Gold;*
Vibrant Colors
LUCKY NUMBER: *1*
LUCKY DAY: *Sunday*

OTHER IMPORTANT LEOS:
Jacqueline Kennedy Onassis
Peter O'Toole
Andy Warhol
Haley Mills
Julia Child
Napoleon
Fidel Castro
Carl Jung
Mae West
Ralph Bunche
Eydie Gorme
Geraldine Chaplin
George Hamilton
Princess Margaret Rose

LEO

GENERAL CHARACTERISTICS

You are a born leader. In you are combined strong feeling and a fine, sensitive intellect. You are frank and you are fair. And you are a real go-getter.

As a Leo, with the brave Lion your symbol, you feel pretty strongly about everything—politics, food, fashions, and other people. Nor are you shy about saying how you feel. You never hesitate to speak out, and while your temper can be a bit sharp at times, you don't brood or carry a grudge.

In other words, "Do, don't stew," might be your motto.

Yours is a fiery Sun-sign personality. You not only attract others instantly, but your lack of self doubt gives them confidence.

Fortunately, you are also kind-hearted and caring. Your own ideas may be pretty fixed (and you can be quite stubborn). Yet you will always give someone else a hearing—or a hand. And when you have made a mistake, you are big enough to admit it and change your course completely if need be.

Your approach to life is full of zest and enthusiasm. People who act bored or negative and "couldn't care less" irritate you immensely. That's because you care so much about everything. You care about doing a good job and making others happy (which you almost always do).

And you care about making the very best of yourself. This is not selfishness so much as a true estimate of your own worth. With a wisdom beyond your age, you know that if you don't like yourself, others won't either. Moreover, this is what gives you such a well defined sense of integrity, for it is true inner confidence rather than bravado. And it is to your credit— at least 99 percent of the time—that you don't take advantage of your power or try to bully others.

You are one of the most independent of the Zodiac signs. You often act like a loner, and like to be the head of anything you do. And yet you have one of the deepest needs to be loved and admired.

In fact, without someone to say "Bravo!" from time to time, you can become moody and difficult. Then the negative part of your

Leo nature comes to the fore. You may act irritable or angry, or you may do something silly, or show off in a flamboyant way. And no one has more deeply hurt feelings than Leo, the Lion, when rejected.

Also, you are really sentimental and romantic. You love to be tender in little ways. And you love to be noticed and to be appreciated.

But even your moody spells never last long. Your normal balance and good humor return, and you can even laugh at yourself afterwards. Perhaps you bounce back more quickly than others because you will always act rather than suffer in silence.

Just one caution to Leo: Because you are a born leader and have such a strong personality, you may on occasion squelch others. You may seem bossy and domineering, which you aren't really. You simply get carried away by haste and your own convictions. Others less forceful may feel slightly crushed, which you can avoid if you make it a point to think of their feelings as much as yours.

Finally, as a Leo, you are extremely inventive. Your creative nature will always opt for the unbroken path, the uncharted course. You decide quickly, and then are persistent in getting where you want to go. And as a Leo, you invariably go far.

PHYSICAL CHARACTERISTICS

You are lucky in health matters. Your constitution is likely to be rugged and you have great reserves of energy. The only real danger to your health is of overdoing. Even a lion can go too fast. Fortunately, you rarely get sick. You fight off illness as if it were an enemy and recuperate quickly from fevers, viruses, and even broken bones. (If you have to be bedridden, you are a terrible patient because you want to be up and moving again. But you'll spring back even quicker if you take your medicine and take care of yourself.)

In looks, Leos have a special dynamic attraction. As a member of this sign, you combine an aristocratic bearing with a vital appeal. And your posture is likely to be excellent.

Leo males are most often the rugged, he-man type, while Leo females usually have fine, slim figures and strong, well-shaped legs. Leo females are very feminine, though not clinging vines, and their eyes are often outstandingly lovely.

In fashion, all Leos love to be first and wear the brightest. Red, gold, and purple are favorite colors. Favorite fabrics are regal, and preferred designs are bold: stripes, Art Nouveau patterns, and free-wheeling plaids. As a Leo, you like accessories with dash, and you never mind being the center of attraction. You are a pace-setter and have the potential to catch everyone's eye at a party, even though you dress to suit yourself.

SCHOOL AND CAREER

IN school, you combine a creative, individual approach to your work with being well organized and efficient. Leos are not grinds, and they work in spurts rather than steadily. But, as a Leo, if you try at all, you are likely to be a top student.

The two problems that may keep you from the honor roll are being too busy with outside activities and not really paying attention. But more likely, you will excel in all directions—academic and extra-curricular. For instance, a Leo male is likely to be captain of the football team *and* president of student council.

Also, as a Leo, you like individual research. You are especially suited to projects where you can act independently. What you write may not be perfectly spelled, but it is bound to be creative.

Many careers are open to Leos. And in whatever you choose—which may be your most difficult job problem—you are likely to lead. Leos are frequently found in the executive suite. And Leo males make excellent engineers, management advisors, and politicians. (Leos not only like to rule, but have great charisma, and would appeal to the voters.)

Leos of both sexes have a flair for the dramatic, and the "born showman" in you might lead you into acting, television, or reporting. Persuasive Leos also are naturally suited to selling.

A Leo female might be a woman's-page editor or a wallpaper designer. She might write, or even pickle beans in her spare time. Whatever she does is likely to be creative, a little different, and successful. But like the Leo male, she may have a hard time sticking to one lifetime job. Her desire for change may lead her to several careers, or to free-lance work which combines a variety of her talents.

MONEY

You like to have plenty of pocket money and you like to splurge occasionally. (You are not naturally suited to slow and steady saving, but you should try to put something aside for a possible rainy day.)

More than others you have a tendency to be constantly and slightly in debt, and this is not a good thing. However, because you are creative and have plenty of drive, you always find a way to make the money you need. Moreover, it would be against your proud nature not to pay your own way.

Lavishness is another minor pitfall. You love to give generous gifts, the biggest and the best. Expensive sports cars and far-out fun furs have a special appeal for you. And when you eat out, you don't like to have to worry about the cost.

Somehow, you spend a lot, yet you work hard and your luck usually runs high. Even some of your foolish speculations turn out to be golden.

And while you are financially overextended from time to time, you are never stingy or selfish where money is concerned. In all ways, you are as generous with others as you are to yourself.

FUN AND LEISURE

LEOS like two kinds of sports primarily—those in which they can be captain of the team, like football and hockey, and those in which they can excel on a personal basis, like skiing, tennis, and swimming.

Skiing especially intrigues Leos because it is fast and exciting, and there is a slight element of danger. For the same reasons, people born under this sign are more fascinated than others by surfing, scuba diving, and horseback riding, particularly on a good, speedy horse.

Leo people do have quieter moments, but even the book they pick up is likely to be an adventure story or a fast-paced mystery. And their preference in records is for rather loud, mind-blasting music, though they would rather see anything live than listen to it second hand.

Leos give the best parties. They are experts at getting others to mix and feel at home. And they always entertain in an unusual, stimulating way. The food, the decorations, and the guests are never run-of-the-mill. (But if you are a Leo, take note that a successful party need not be a lavish one, for sometimes you get carried away by your own plans.)

Leo is the Sun-ruled sign, and all Leos love to travel, especially to follow the sun from a sun-struck ski slope in winter to a bright beach in summer. Leo travelers find excitement wherever they go, but thrive on the unusual—like going around the world on a tramp steamer or being the first to sail somewhere on a small boat.

HOME AND FAMILY

LEOs are independent, but they do not like to live alone. At heart, they are one of the most people-geared of any of the signs.

As a Leo you love your home and love to be in it. It is just the place you need in order to rest and be refreshed. You value your privacy, though you are also generous with your time if a family member calls.

You prefer to have a room of your own and prize your possessions highly—not because they are valuable but because of sentimental reasons. They remind you of a place or a person or a happy time. Moreover, though you are not naturally neat, you are a born collector— anything from owls to seashells to pop posters.

In family relationships, you are fiercely loyal. But you may be a bit bossy with non-Leo brothers and sisters. You make them toe the line, perhaps a bit too much. All your relationships will be smoother if you learn to share the limelight, as well as the television set and the most comfortable chair.

You love your parents as people but sometimes resent their authority. You may also think they are a bit behind the times. Occasionally you have a point, but you will prove it better by reasoning than arguing. And you should learn to listen, which is always a little hard for a Leo.

FRIENDSHIP

You are very affectionate and care deeply for your friends, of which you have many, both close and casual. With them, you are dynamic and take the dominant lead. Socially, there is nothing passive about you. You lead; others follow.

Yet sometimes your friends find you a little hard to figure out. The uncertainty is in approaching you. Sometimes you can seem distant and hard to reach, whereas other times you are warm, outgoing, and full of fun. Both the regal and the sunny are parts of the Leo nature, just as the Lion, the king of beasts, is an aloof, solitary creature at times and a happy, playful beast at other times. And this is the apparent contradiction which adds depth to your personality but occasionally baffles your friends. One day you are intimate and close; the next you shut yourself off. Your good friends know that either way you act, your caring for them remains steadfast and true—for you are one of the most loyal of all the signs.

Throughout life, you make friends easily.

Your hand is quick to reach out and your humor is ready. And going to a party where you "don't know a soul" never bothers you. Rather, it is a challenge that appeals to your Leo nature.

You like to organize your friends, and are likely to be the leader of any group you are in (though you are also likely to spread yourself wider and to have friends in many groups). Sometimes a good friend doesn't want to change his ways to suit you. But any difficulty in this direction usually irons itself out easily because you are excellent at communicating when there is a problem—and you are sympathetic. Furthermore, you know the art of disagreeing with another person while continuing to like him or her personally.

Sometimes you handle things almost too well, and your own great sensitivity is covered up by your ability to cope. Your stalwart front hides a deep Leo fear of loneliness. And yet you shouldn't worry, for no one better excels in the art of friendship than warm-hearted, fiery Leo.

ROMANCE

LOVE means more to a Leo than to others. Anyone of this sign has a "presence" that makes itself known to the opposite sex. Leo's approach to love is vibrant and exciting, yet always personal.

Others care deeply, but as a Leo your caring tends to be all-consuming, like the elemental fire of your sign. Yet you also like to do the little things for the one you are interested in. You enjoy writing letters, making frequent phone calls, and giving and receiving presents. And you are likely to build up a "just us" storehouse of jokes, pet names, and pastimes.

Faking feeling is one thing you cannot do. Nor can you care seriously about two people at the same time. What you *can* do is really like one person but still flirt with others. You are not even trying to make the person you care about jealous. It's just that it would be unthinkable for you to go to a party and talk only to one person. Sometimes you can't help being the center of attention.

On the other hand, if your feelings change and a new person comes into your life, you will not hesitate to break up an old romance. Such frankness may be hard on an old flame, but it usually works out better in the long run.

The Leo male leads, in love as in life. He feels like a king and that's the way he wants to be treated. Therefore, his preference is usually for a very feminine, clinging sort of girl who will adore him and go along with his every wish. (Underneath, he may be a soft touch and give in easily when there is any difference, but on the surface he wants his wishes respected and obeyed.)

Since loyalty is one of his outstanding characteristics, he is essentially a one-girl person— at least one girl at a time. He is also deeply tender and sensitive to his date's moods and feelings. What occasionally seems gruff and quick in his manner is only a cover up for his own feelings and a fear of being hurt. His pride is so great that it takes him far longer than others to recuperate from a broken romance.

The Leo female is equally sensitive and romantic. She loves to be treated like a queen. She gives her feelings wholly and cares completely for the object of her affection. She is the one who will spend hours searching for just the right tie or cooking a complicated dish because *he* likes it. She is spontaneous and generous and totally idealistic. Emotion, not reason, rules her romantically, and she is lucky that her intuition is good and she usually chooses wisely.

COMPATIBILITY GUIDE

WITH ARIES: You are both proud and energetic. But two born leaders are likely to clash. As your personalities are equally fiery and possessive, the only hope for a lasting relationship is if you both curb your temper and your will to dominate. If you can work things out, there should be a lot of exciting times together.

WITH TAURUS: Leo is always on the go while Taurus prefers to stay in the background. But you are both affectionate and considerate. Taurus may be just the sort of clinging vine that vibrant Leo is looking for. So in spite of personality differences, the two of you could make a positive go of it.

WITH GEMINI: This relationship should be anything but dull. Gemini rather intrigues Leo, because it's hard to pin a Geminian down—which makes an exciting romantic challenge for Leo. You also have a lot in common: a real zest for life, many outside interests, and bright, gregarious personalities. The possibilities are, in fact, terrific.

WITH CANCER: Cancer moodiness and supersensitivity may irritate more easygoing Leo. Without thinking, Leo is likely to hurt Cancer's fragile feelings. A successful relationship is possible, but it will take a lot of true give and take. Tact, and a touch of tenderness, is needed here.

WITH LEO: People born under the same sign have a tendency to ignore each other completely, or they are strongly, almost magnetically, attracted to each other. If the latter is true, don't fight it—but do watch what you say. Otherwise little clashes are likely to build into long, hot arguments. Also, both must curb that competitive spirit.

WITH VIRGO: This may be a case of opposites attract, for Virgo is as practical and careful as Leo is fancy free and spendthrift. On the other hand, Virgo may point out faults Leo would rather ignore, and Leo may be a little too boisterous for quieter Virgo. Thus, the relationship can be complementary—or one where there is constant bickering.

WITH LIBRA: The two of you should make a happy, responsive team. With love, Libra's level-headed qualities will temper but not put out Leo's fire. Your likes and dislikes are similar and you both have a deep and yearning need for affection. You should be a most attractive and vital combination.

WITH SCORPIO: There's a strong attraction between Leo and Scorpio. But watch out, things may not be just what they seem. A Scorpio usually has a lot of secrets. And a Leo is not always good at looking at the situation objectively. One of you is likely to be more serious than the other. You both are strong-minded. Just be sure it's about the same thing.

WITH SAGITTARIUS: One of the most fulfilling and fun-loving relationships is possible when you two get together. You are both Fire signs. You both are also outgoing, romantic, and a little happy-go-lucky. This stimulating relationship could only be marred by too possessive an attitude on either person's part.

WITH CAPRICORN: Slow and steady is the Capricorn pace. But it is not Leo's. However, any Capricorn person has wisdom and just the kind of thoughtful ways the headstrong Leo temperament sometimes needs. If you respect each other as well as like each other, you should be able to work things out—possibly quite stunningly.

WITH AQUARIUS: Both of you are freedom loving and yet have strong, ardent natures. The only problem may be that Aquarius loves the whole world while Leo wants a strong one-person relationship. Success may depend on whether Leo can convince Aquarius to give up some independence, which Aquarius will do only if he or she feels this is really "it."

WITH PISCES: Pisces' personality is likely to be too leisurely and dreamy for always-on-the-go Leo. Loving togetherness is possible (because underneath you fascinate each other), but only if the more dominant Leo is careful not to swamp his Pisces partner's basically shy nature.

VIRGO

★ *August 22 - September 22* ★

ELEMENT: *Earth*
RULED BY: *Mercury*
SYMBOL: *Virgin*
KEY WORD: *Capable*
JEWEL: *Diamond*
COLORS: *Gray, Violet, Yellow-Green;*
Muted Tones
LUCKY NUMBER: *5*
LUCKY DAY: *Tuesday*

OTHER IMPORTANT VIRGOS:

Lauren Becall
Anne Bancroft
Ingrid Bergman
Leonard Bernstein
Maurice Chevalier
Henry Ford II
Elia Kazan
Carol Lawrence
Roy Wilkins
Romy Schneider
David McCallum
Sophia Loren
Lyndon B. Johnson

VIRGO

GENERAL CHARACTERISTICS

You are intellectual and an idealist. What you really want is perfection, and so you sometimes seem hard on others—and on yourself.

Keenly articulate, you know where you are going and just how to express yourself. And you enjoy conversation. The exchange of ideas excites and stimulates you.

Integrity is your standard, and you won't settle for white lies or halfway measures. You are completely honest in your dealings with others, and concerning money. Moreover, you like to be sure. You are not a born chance-taker.

But you *are* a born worker. You are energetic and ambitious, and usually successful in whatever you undertake. You tackle any job with enthusiasm, and with a practical "let's see it work" attitude. There is nothing superficial or haphazard about the way you operate. You are thorough and methodical, and your decisions are made by thinking rather than by feeling.

You are sometimes reserved, and you like a quiet, well-ordered life. But you are not really shy. It is just that you are not readily demonstrative in showing your affection. For you are capable of deep feeling. And you are completely committed to your family and friends. Even in romance you combine mental detachment with the capacity for intense personal feeling.

Devotion and loyalty are strong in your nature. You have to know and examine all the facts before you take up a cause or person. But once you have decided, you are unswerving. Your faith never falters.

Bent on self-improvement, you are always taking a course or going on a diet or taking up something new. This is because you are never fully satisfied with yourself. You command admiration and respect from others because you seem so self-confident and speak so well. You are the only one who is not fully convinced of your worth, for underneath you are full of self-doubts. You wonder "Can I make it?"

The answer is "Of course you can." But you must try to temper your critical nature, and learn to be less exacting. You must also accept other people and circumstances as they are and not continuously try to change the world.

By such acceptance, and by not constantly picking at the negative, you will free the fine positive powers of your thinking.

PHYSICAL CHARACTERISTICS

YOUR health is naturally good and you take good care of yourself. Because of that, you usually prevent illness from getting a strong hold on you. And even when you are occasionally ill, you take your medicine and do as the doctor says. You don't like to be ill and want it over with as quickly as possible.

If, on the other hand, you do not get enough rest or wear yourself out through overdoing, you are likely to suffer from "nerves," which will probably affect your stomach. Only occasionally does a Virgo become so preoccupied with his or her health that he or she becomes a hypochondriac, always talking about physical troubles and always seeking sympathy for illnesses which are, for the most part, imaginary.

By far the greater number of Virgos are not only in surprising good health, but have the ability to look and feel young throughout life.

Virgos are good-looking types, with features that are regular and on the small side. Virgo females are often exceptionally beautiful and rather regal. Virgo males have an active, energetic appearance and strong masculine appeal.

In dress, you are always well turned out. Your appearance is tidy and everything matches. And you prefer the practical: clothes that last a long time and really work. Your slacks are for walking in, not just being looked at, and you buy a bathing suit for serious swimming, not merely because it is the latest fad. And you prefer to have a few good suits, coats, and dresses rather than a closet full of inexpensive items.

You are an Earth sign, and this influences your choices. You are happiest in greens and browns, and also like red, soft blue, and pumpkin orange. Stripes and small prints appeal to Virgo's sense of order, whether in a tie or a dress.

SCHOOL AND CAREER

YOUR natural mental brightness combined with your efficiency and fine organization mean that school is generally smooth sailing for you. Furthermore, you like what you are doing, and you are less bothered than most signs by long assignments or research projects. You are even good at allotting time, so you do not get caught in frantic last-minute rushes.

On the other hand, you are uncomfortable if you are not prepared. Because of this, surprise quizzes and spontaneous questions in class are far more likely to throw you than an assignment you can prepare and plan ahead of time.

You are a thoughtful and fine speaker, and are likely to be found on debating teams or student councils.

Later, you will be equally dedicated to your work, and proud of it. It may take you longer than most to make a decision that "This is for me." But once decided, you are not likely to change. You do your shopping around first, and then are apt to stay put.

Virgos have natural executive ability. They know how to handle people and make decisions, and how to size up a situation, no matter how complex.

You also have a strong critical ability, and drama critics, reporters, and stock market analysts are frequently Virgos. Since you like to impart knowledge, you might be a teacher or a scientist.

Male Virgos are often found in legal or financial fields. (You are both impartial and fair.)

Female Virgos are especially suited to be executive secretaries, authors, and interior decorators, or to be in businesses like television or catering. You are suited to anything that demands planning and perseverance—plus your own personal, creative touch.

MONEY

You are careful about money and uncomfortable when you don't have "a penny in your pocket." You are also good at handling money, and know the value of saving.

Sometimes you would like to splurge, and occasionally do, but it is against your basic nature. And you rarely buy anything on time.

Having enough money is important to you, not because you like to show off, but because it makes you feel secure. In fact, having enough money means that you don't worry about it. If for any reason you are strapped, you feel anxious and nervous and aren't free to do your best. But usually you take on a summer or part-time or after-school job to make sure this does not happen.

And when you spend, it is mainly for necessities or to please others. You like quality more than quantity, but an item does not have to be expensive or "in" to delight you. The main thing is whether it "works," or serves its purpose. You couldn't care less about impressing others, for even your financial standards are internal—and based on soundness and integrity.

FUN AND LEISURE

You like sports—almost all kinds—and the more active the better. But you prefer to be right in there rather than on the sidelines, and you prefer team sports to solitary ones.

Virgo males are found on football, baseball, and soccer teams. (The Virgo male has a keen sense of strategy, and is frequently captain.)

Virgo females prefer team swimming, hockey, bowling, and tennis. They are energetic and agile, and play a "thinking" game as well as a strong one.

Virgos of both sexes are also intellectual, and love card games, movies, and live theater. And they enjoy games, solving problems, and putting together puzzles more than any other sign.

In books, the preference is for adventure and also poetry (which fits the Virgo nature because exacting forms are pleasing). In records Virgos incline toward the classics and toward cool jazz and rock. A too-blaring beat both bothers and bores the calm, calculated Virgo temperament.

You love to entertain, but want the house to be in order and everything shipshape. And you prefer a planned party to people just dropping in (which sometimes throws you into fussiness and makes you uncomfortable). You, and others, would have more fun if you could relax and be a little more spontaneous. Carefree fun means more than having everything "just so." But you need and want people around you, and you have the ability and charm to be a fine host or hostess.

Traveling doesn't mean a great deal to you. You prefer to stay close to home base. But a change does anyone good, and you are interested in exploring other places and in meeting new people. Again, you prefer the planned trip to the spontaneous excursion, and you always make sure you leave with enough money to meet any emergency.

HOME AND FAMILY

HARMONIOUS conditions mean a great deal to you, and you like to live in a restful, agreeable atmosphere.

On the other hand, you sometimes find it

hard to agree with other family members because you may feel your way of life is the only one, and your style may be more exacting than that of others under the same roof.

Irrational or emotional behavior annoys you, and sometimes you cut others close to you short rather than really try to understand their viewpoint.

You are rarely aggressive, but if criticized by a parent or older brother or sister, you can become sullen and resentful. This is partly because your thinking is certain, but your feelings about yourself are doubtful. When you are really sure of yourself, you find it easy to understand another's viewpoint, even if it is quite different from your own.

You are a person who needs the security of a solid family behind you, and, in turn, you are loyal to them. You also take pride in your home and in your own room, which is as neat and orderly and well-organized as you are.

Younger brothers and sisters look up to you, and you rarely get into serious trouble at home. But you do tend to brood, and you want to please loved ones so much that you don't always please yourself. This kind of self-sacrifice takes its toll, and you eventually become resentful. Relax and give in to your basically temperate, good nature—this is Virgo's clue to a happy home life.

FRIENDSHIP

OTHERS sometimes think you are timid, but you are really more discriminating than shy in your choice of close friends. (On the other hand, you have many acquaintances, and are always eager to enlarge your circle.)

Usually, you gravitate to people who are as aggressive, intelligent, and progressive as you are. And you thoroughly enjoy the art of conversation. You can talk for hours long into the night when you find a soul mate.

You are a loyal friend, and you will do a good turn for anyone who has befriended you. But you do expect something in return. And if anyone lets you down, you will let him or her know it. Then you can be as momentarily sharp as you are basically generous. This is because of your great need to be appreciated. For you are not really self-effacing. Rather, you long secretly for recognition and the limelight.

Sometimes you overestimate thinking, and your logical approach can annoy and exasperate close friends who are more emotionally geared. It is hard for you to believe that not everything can be proved. Yet you have a keen intuitive sense, if you will only let it come to the fore. And you must never be so busy thinking that you have no time to feel. For you are not really cold or authoritarian. Underneath you are a kind and caring friend—and no one makes a better one than you. Left alone you falter, but with others you grow, and the positive parts of your Virgo personality take the dominant role.

ROMANCE

You seem inhibited, but are really very affectionate. Yours is a cool aloofness and a special kind of charm. Though you express yourself delicately, sometimes even shyly, you show real finesse in romance. You do not "come on strong," but stay in the mind long after a lighter, more casual interest has faded.

You rarely fall in love at first sight. Mental compatibility generally comes first, and you are likely to know a person for a long time before becoming serious. Commitment for you is an important and well thought out step. You never give your heart casually or make false promises.

On the other hand, you do like to flirt, and are apt to have a lot of light romantic flings before deciding on "the" one. For one thing, you enjoy the company of the opposite sex—talking and probing another person's mind. But you also want to examine many alternatives and know all kinds of people before you get too deeply involved. This makes you an easy person to get to know, but a hard person to get to know well. And you are likely to run away if the person interested in you is too dominant or demonstrative, which embarrasses you and makes you feel you don't have much in common.

But you really are affectionate, and are capable of deep love. You are also generous and tender and caring—unless put on the defensive. Then you can be critical, and tend to expect your loved one to live up to impossible ideals. When you are sure of his or her feelings, your natural good nature returns. Thus, it is important to talk out any differences—quickly and completely—before an insignificant incident widens into a deep, romantic rift.

The Virgo male is thoughtful and wants to please. But his seeming reserve may be a bit baffling. Often this is because it is hard for him to reveal his innermost thoughts and feelings— at least until he is sure of you, and of himself. Once he has made up his mind, he is as unreserved in giving his love as he was formerly secretive about showing it. He may have some fixed ideas, but he is always an interesting companion and is faithful and loyal in love.

The Virgo female longs for someone to care about. She loves to listen to her loved one, to comfort and aid and do things for him. She is a delightful partner in any project and is a lively foil for her date's ideas. At first meeting she may seem distant, but she responds warmly and fully when she feels loved. And love to her always means security and a future. So she is likely to have many romances before settling down to the one who truly loves and understands her. Sometimes she may seem cold and fault-finding—but this is only because it is a basically wrong relationship. And sensing this, she becomes less than her best Virgo self.

COMPATIBILITY GUIDE

WITH ARIES: Aries' love of adventure might antagonize stay-at-home Virgo—while Virgo's perfectionist ways might make Aries want to be even more on the go. Nevertheless, these two unlike people can work out a happy alliance, and intellectual likenesses could bridge a basic emotional gap.

WITH TAURUS: Many characteristics in common should lead to compatibility. Taurus is so easygoing and good-natured that even Virgo's occasional fault-finding doesn't faze him or her. You are both romantic, yet practical. Together, you balance and blend, because the only differences are superficial.

WITH GEMINI: Your minds work in different ways. Gemini is impulsive and rather unstable, while Virgo is well organized and plans ahead. Nevertheless, you intrigue each other. Gemini's swift mood changes soften Virgo's rigidity, and Virgo gives flighty Gemini a feeling of roots and stability.

WITH CANCER: Virgo is a sympathetic partner for Cancer's lonesome or blue moods. But Virgo must avoid too much advice-giving, or Cancer will withdraw and become hurt. This can be a constructive relationship if Virgo tempers the urge to reform with humor and patience. Deep, lasting affection is possible if you both really want to please.

WITH LEO: The reserved, sometimes aloof attitude of Virgo may annoy and "turn off" proud, passionate-feeling Leo. On the other hand, Virgo may have a secret yearning to break loose. Leo's intensity and excitement may be just the thing to free Virgo's feelings. Yours could be just a disinterested friendship, but the possibilities are positive—and may be surprising.

WITH VIRGO: There may not be much spark here since you both are basically undemonstrative and reserved. In other words, it is hard for you to "light each other's fire." However, if you

are both positive types and willing to adapt—
and make a real effort—yours could be a delightfully happy and rich alliance.

WITH LIBRA: Libra is somewhat spendthrift in nature and lives in the present, while Virgo is basically thrifty and plans for the future. The two of you won't see eye-to-eye on a lot of things, and it will take a lot of tact and understanding on both parts to make this relationship successful. Still and all, there is a definite underlying appeal.

WITH SCORPIO: This should be quite a team, since both of you are industrious, energetic people. You should get a lot done and enjoy doing it together. But you both are natural "pickers," and must be careful not to nag or belittle each other.

WITH SAGITTARIUS: You both move swiftly, and flexible Sagittarius is a perfect balance for Virgo's tendency to have everything "just so." Also, you both have a strong spirit of play and humor, and you both love to entertain and have fun. Delightful companionship and deep mutual respect make this a fine combination.

WITH CAPRICORN: You strongly interest each other and should be happy together. You are both capable and considerate, and like an orderly way of life. Both of you are down to earth, and like to plan and dream ahead. But the relationship is far from dull, for both of you are also affectionate and thoroughly enjoy life.

WITH AQUARIUS: Aquarius' range takes in humanity and the whole world, while Virgo prefers to stay near home base. Therefore, Aquarius will be on the go a great deal and Virgo is likely to feel neglected. A strong bond is likely to develop only if there is real communication from the start. The attraction is genuine, but the outlook is undecided.

WITH PISCES: Pisces loves to shower attention on others, which is just what Virgo needs to break out of his or her shell. And Virgo gives unsure Pisces a feeling of security. Your tastes may be quite different but your basic temperaments are a lot alike, and in the deepest way, you answer each other's needs.

LIBRA

★ *September 23 - October 22* ★

ELEMENT: *Air*
RULED BY: *Venus*
SYMBOL: *Scales*
KEY WORD: *Understanding*
JEWEL: *Emerald*
COLORS: *Blue, Light Green, Off-White;*
Soothing Tones
LUCKY NUMBER: *6*
LUCKY DAY: *Friday*

OTHER IMPORTANT LIBRAS:
Julie Andrews
Pope Paul VI
Brigitte Bardot
Truman Capote
T. S. Eliot
Helen Hayes
Groucho Marx
Charles H. Percy
Gore Vidal
Ed Sullivan
Anthony Newley
Melina Mercouri
Vladimir Horowitz
Dwight D. Eisenhower

LIBRA

LOVE of harmony pervades everything you do. You like things to be in balance, yourself included. You are extremely fair and just, and you sympathize with anyone who is troubled or oppressed.

Sometimes you seem to take a long time to make up your mind. This is because you weigh all the pros and cons before coming to any decision. Moreover, you can see all sides to a question. You may seem to waver when you are merely trying to make a decision without prejudice.

You love company and are seldom alone. And you have a real talent for getting along with people, for you are not only kind, but caring about others' feelings. Generally your temper is even. You seldom flare up or say anything rash. And even if you do, your bad mood is quickly over, and you don't hold a grudge.

Beautiful and artistic things matter to you,

and you lean toward the luxurious rather than the plain. Sometimes it would be better if you could be a bit more practical, for you tend to get carried away. You want things you cannot have, and become depressed and secretly unhappy when brought back to reality. You are easily hurt, and can become quite disagreeable, when you don't get the attention you think you deserve.

But most of the time your ways are easygoing and your manners are excellent. No one has better tact, and you know how to please by dropping a compliment or doing a favor. And you always remember to write thank-you notes.

You are extremely sensitive to ugliness and to anything disturbing. At times you may be called squeamish, and can even become ill at the sight or smell of something unpleasant. (This is especially true of Libra females, who have such a highly tuned sense of the beautiful that anything out of kilter disturbs their whole nervous system.)

Only occasionally does the Libra desire for the true and the beautiful turn into snobbery. In such cases, the lesser-type Libra is likely to thrive on gossip, feeling basically somewhat superior. Moreover, the thoughtful, somewhat analytical talk of even the positive Libra can become, in this case, smooth talk, and a kind of cleverness that comes close to deceit.

Most Libras are of the positive type. They are not only pleasant, but have a delightful wit and a strong, probing sense of curiosity. They are renowned for their diplomacy and intelligence—which, combined with their affectionate nature, makes them people other people want to know.

PHYSICAL CHARACTERISTICS

Your general constitution is good and your ways are usually temperate. You suffer mainly when you are thrown off balance. This can happen due to illness or to a case of nerves, for feelings and thoughts affect you internally and can upset you to the point of making you sick. This happens most often if you come across ugliness or are disillusioned—for it is harder for you to "take" harsh or difficult circumstances than it is for other signs.

You should beware of cold and dampness because you tend to take cold easily. However, this is less likely to happen if you get enough rest (Libras like to stay late at parties) and watch your diet (sometimes your love of food clashes with your desire to stay thin).

When you are ill, you want plenty of attention. It is not in your nature to suffer in silence.

Luckily, you are not really as delicate as you sometimes seem. The Libra male especially often has an outstanding vitality and inner strength.

Both males and females are poised, rather elegant types, with good posture and well-balanced regular features. Both have exceptional charm and sex appeal. Moreover, you are always well-dressed and well-groomed. And Libra females are noted for their soft, musical voices and smooth complexions.

In clothes, Libra females love elegance, soft fabrics, and rich colors. You are likely to wear clothes well and you are concerned with the total look of your outfit. You love accessories and jewelry, and wear scarves with a flair. Lavender, pastel blue, yellow, and soft red are favorite colors.

The Libra male knows what's "in." And whatever it is, he's first in wearing it. Rugged, semi-casual clothes please him most, and he wears even tennis shoes and tee-shirts with style and dash.

SCHOOL AND CAREER

As a Libra you have excellent mental powers, but you tend to let things slide. You can make good grades if you feel like it, but too many outside activities frequently tempt you. Your attention wanders and you put off homework assignments until the last minute. This is too bad, because with a little effort you could be at the top of your class.

You excel in anything that demands analysis. Philosophy is your special meat, and you can argue both the pros and cons. And when you make a value judgment, you do it with complete detachment. You may personally feel one way, but you can appreciate another person's way of thinking.

Your range of understanding is wide. And even involved subjects like chemistry and higher mathematics don't "throw" you as they do others. You also know how to put knowledge into perspective, which is why you are better at long essay-type tests rather than tests with questions that depend on quick, factual competence.

Because you have a keen mind and the ability to see things a number of ways, you would make an excellent lawyer, teacher, or critic. And your deep yet detached understanding suits you for social or rehabilitation work, or to be a psychologist or psychiatrist. The Peace Corps, or other work connected with a cause, would also appeal.

Libra males might be drawn to investment

and banking circles, and because they have such convincing ways, they make top-notch salesmen. Pharmacist and scientist are other career possibilities for the Libra male. They are not, however, fond of cut-throat competition, and prefer professional and small-business setups to huge concerns with a "dog eat dog" atmosphere.

Libra females might be found in any of the above fields, and also in the arts. You yourself may be an artist or designer, or interested in a job touching on cosmetics or the home. And there are many famous Libra models. With your charm, the opportunities will be as abundant as your varied talents.

MONEY

You will never be the type to concentrate on making money. But you do enjoy using it, for you love luxury and quality and anything artistic. Libra females like real jewelry and well-designed clothes, while Libra males have a weakness for good sports cars, sports equipment, and camping gear.

Still and all, though your attitude to making money is easygoing, you somehow always have enough. Maybe that's because you think things out so clearly before you make a move—such as taking on a job or making an investment.

Your main money problem is simply that you want more than you can afford, and you can't stick to a budget. You also find it almost impossible to save. To you a penny earned is a penny spent—and often before it has even warmed your pocket!

It is in your favor that you love the pleasures of life and are so responsive—as well as generous to others. But it is always a good idea to have something put away. This would increase your sense of well-being as well as your bank account.

FUN AND LEISURE

You are not as active in sports as those born under some signs. Mainly, this is because you just don't have the time—not with all your social interests and other activities.

However, you are extremely well-coordinated. You are good at all sports, but excel in those where speed is important: skiing, track, tennis, hockey, and basketball. You have a strong team spirit and know how to cooperate for the good of the group. You don't have to be the "star" to do your best.

Often Libra females do not go in for heavy sports, but prefer to take up ballet, horseback riding, or form swimming. They are exceptionally graceful, which also suits them to figure skating.

Libras of both sexes enjoy almost any pastime as long as they can do it with someone. Bicycle-riding, going to a foreign film, belonging to a camera club, or trying a new restaurant are activities you would particularly enjoy.

In books and records, your tastes cover the field, from classics to the best-seller list and the "top ten." Your main wish is to have someone with whom you can talk over what you have read or heard.

Parties are your thing. You love to give them and go to them, and the more people the merrier. And while you would just as soon go to a picnic as a ball, you prefer there to be some touch of artistry: wild flowers on the table, decorations on the potato salad, and your jeans artfully fringed. And while you like large, convivial groups, you do not like noisy, raucous ones—and you are completely turned off by rudeness, offensive jokes, and rough behavior.

You are an Air sign. As such, you like to go anywhere the wind blows. To always stay home is as unnatural for you as to be alone. But you are more likely to take short trips and to go off on a weekend in the country than to take

one long trip. That's because you enjoy leaving
—and coming back.

HOME AND FAMILY

You like harmony in the house as in other
phases of your life. You can't stand an atmosphere of constant discord and upset. Sometimes you will even say "yes" when you really
mean "no" just to keep the peace—which only
leads to later difficulties, because eventually you
have to backtrack and say what you really
mean.

If yours is a large family, you may feel annoyed by the inevitable noise and clutter. You
may long to escape the confusion of your home
surroundings, without even trying to speak up
and remedy the situation. Your desire for elegance and beauty is so strong that you can't
stand things being in a shambles or in disrepair.
If you share a room with a non-Libra brother
or sister, there may be constant friction, with
you either becoming picky or pulling back into
a sensitive, withdrawn shell.

To be casual is not necessarily to be careless,
and you will enjoy your home if you are less of
a perfectionist about it. However, whatever
touches you add will enhance, and mothers do

well to listen to the decorating advice of their Libra daughters.

Sometimes, however, you do not like to take the advice of your parents. This may be partly because, as a Libra, you swing this way, then that way in your own ideas.

Also, when you do not communicate, they have a hard time figuring out how you really feel. And sometimes you stew rather than really think things out.

Your parents know you better than you sometimes think. They try to encourage your creative powers but at the same time give you a sense of discipline that can nudge aimless wandering into a worthwhile life path.

Basically, affection is deep between family members, and you are in closer harmony than you sometimes think.

FRIENDSHIP

You are a generous, fine friend, and you will have many casual and close friends throughout life. It is easy for you to make new friends, for you are not shy about speaking to a new person or going to parties where you don't know anyone. You, of all signs, will take the new boy or girl in school under your wing.

You are also always ready to replace the old with the new, and this applies as much to the people you know as to the clothes you wear. But when you drop someone, you do it with tact and without any hint of meanness. You may be a little unreliable, and are more than a little unpredictable. Still and all, you are a generous and thoughtful friend. And you are exceptionally considerate. You remember birthdays and a person's likes and pet peeves as well as the more formal aspects of politeness. You also remember to ask a friend how he or she feels, and then you listen, really listen, to what is said in response.

You have a rather quick temper, but never stay angry long. And you hate to hurt anyone's feelings. Occasionally, though, your inner feelings may be a lot more stirred up than your outward behavior indicates. You are not quite so cool and unflappable as you try to seem. In fact, you may, even though rarely, say something unkind behind a person's back while seeming to be friendly in front of that person. In such a case, it is better to bring any difference out into the open rather than bury it—because it won't stay buried and will niggle at you until you say or do something unbecoming to your basic Libra self. In other words, your only problem concerning friends is expressing what you feel before it builds into any lasting resentment.

ROMANCE

YOUR romantic nature is the most intense of any of the signs. This comes naturally, since your ruling planet is Venus.

Although you are detached in your general thinking, when it comes to romance, your reaction is warm and strictly personal. You also have a unique and creative flair where love is concerned. When you care for someone, you instinctively know just the right romantic gesture to please and the right words to turn "maybe" into "yes."

While your interest is always strong, it is often of the moment, and it is likely to change from one person to another. With you, a romance is red-hot—but only as long as it lasts. Another pretty or handsome face can change the scene in an instant. (However, you feel terrible if anyone turns the romantic tables on you, for your intensity also shows in your jealous and sometimes overpossessive attitude.)

But your sentimentality about little things and your basic consideration charms almost everyone you meet. And even though you are not likely to be constant in your devotion, you always let another down with such tact that he or she is enriched by knowing you rather than shattered by a romantic failure.

Libra males thrive on appreciation. And they know how to make a girl feel very special and very feminine. Moreover, they are considerate of her feelings. If basketball is not her greatest love and opera is, the Libra male will go occasionally—just to please her.

But just because Libra males are loyal while interested does not mean that their interest is constant. It is quite the opposite. They are likely to have many short-lived but quite intense romances before becoming really serious.

Once they have decided, it will likely be for good, and the relationship will be exceedingly long-lasting and happy. That's because they have searched the field and made sure beforehand.

The Libra female is known as a charmer. It is easy for her to twist almost any male around her finger, and it is hard to imagine her without a romantic interest. In fact, without romance, she feels that something is missing in her life.

She, too, is inclined to be fickle until she finds the "real" thing. But she is an interesting companion and a harmonious, easygoing date who is a delight even if she is not around as long as others. She is so feminine she gives the impression of being delicate (though she is a strong person underneath). She loves to be protected, and can always find someone more than willing to do the job. And when she does finally know where her heart lies, she will be as devoted and constant as before she was fickle.

COMPATIBILITY GUIDE

WITH ARIES: You are both affectionate, and have a wide variety of interests in common. Still, the relationship may not run smoothly. Aries may seem self-centered and want to dominate. The quick Aries temper may make Libra unhappy. And Libra may become jealous, which only makes matters worse. Consideration and Libra tact are needed to make you click.

WITH TAURUS: Taurus is more practical than luxury-loving Libra, and Taurus' realistic approach to life may clash with Libra idealism. But there's a strong basic attraction, and since you both are agreeable people, the relationship should be relatively trouble free.

WITH GEMINI: There is bound to be a lot of mutual mental stimulation in this twosome. You not only have a lot of friends, but a lot of friends in common. And the excitable Gemini nature will be tempered by the calmer Libra. Your ability to communicate should solve any minor problems.

WITH CANCER: Cancer is emotional, and the Cancer moodiness may baffle and exasperate the steadier Libra. But as long as Libra keeps his or her self-confidence, the possibilities are positive. And the Libra composure is just what unsteady Cancer needs. Another plus is that you both love the arts.

WITH LEO: You will get along fine if Libra curbs his or her tongue and doesn't try to tell Leo what to do. Much can be done through warm mutual appreciation. Since Leo is the dramatic sign of the Zodiac, let Leo have center stage. Libra may really rule, but it must be from the sidelines, and with kindness.

WITH VIRGO: A good relationship is possible, but is not likely to happen right off the bat. At first Virgo seems stand-offish, reserved, and overcritical. Virgo may not supply Libra's great need for affection and encouragement. But you both have the same inner longings for security and love. With some adjustment you will both be very happy.

WITH LIBRA: You share the same ideas and ideals. You have a great mutual need for harmony. The only problems accur in times of discord. One or both of you may withdraw. Then stubborn, hurt pride marks misunderstandings worse than they really are. It is important to remember that giving up does not need to be the same as giving in.

WITH SCORPIO: Libra is likely to have a strong attraction to emotional Scorpio. But Scorpio is a hard person to know well, and a successful relationship will demand all of Libra's natural tact and tolerance. You may wound each other's feelings, but both of you feel deeply, and if you feel deeply about each other, you should solve any difficulties.

WITH SAGITTARIUS: The camaraderie should be delightful! Even minor arguments will be lively and have a touch of humor. And the compatibility is likely to endure because you are both generous and deeply caring people. But Libra should take care never to make freedom-loving Sagittarius feel hemmed in.

WITH CAPRICORN: Capricorn may be too restrained for more outgoing Libra. Libra may even feel frustrated and rejected. But Capricorn can be fun loving, and is not as serious as he or she seems. It takes all the Libra tact and understanding to take the "if" out of this relationship.

WITH AQUARIUS: There should be harmony

of spirit. You give each other mental compatibility, and are both generous, affectionate types. You are both popular and have many shared interests. As long as neither of you becomes possessive, there should be few problems—for you both have strong inborn senses of personal freedom, which must not be infringed upon.

WITH PISCES: Pisces is evasive and may be hard for Libra to pin down. In other words, it is hard to reach the inner Pisces person. But Libra loves a challenge and is deft at delving and understanding. In spite of basic emotional differences, and with effort on both sides, this should be a fine, although rather quiet, relationship.

SCORPIO

★ *October 23 - November 22* ★

ELEMENT: *Water*
RULED BY: *Pluto*
SYMBOL: *Scorpion*
KEY WORD: *Intense*
JEWEL: *Coral*
COLORS: *Brown, Green, Aqua, Coral;*
Murky Hues
LUCKY NUMBER: *9*
LUCKY DAY: *Tuesday*

OTHER IMPORTANT SCORPIOS:
Richard Burton
Dylan Thomas
Mahalia Jackson
Robert F. Kennedy
Princess Grace
Walter Cronkite
Katharine Hepburn
James Jones
Burt Lancaster
Mike Nichols
Pablo Picasso
Joan Sutherland
Roy Campanella
Art Carney

SCORPIO

GENERAL CHARACTERISTICS

You are one of the most intense of any of the signs. Sometimes you seem self-contained. But underneath your apparent calm are seething and contradictory depths.

Certainly there is nothing simple about knowing you. Nor is it in your nature to reveal yourself completely. You are honest and "lay your cards on the table." But you never quite lay out all of them. You always keep some fact, some surprising characteristic, in reserve.

Yours is a unique charm, partly based on this underlying sense of mystery. Also, you yourself are fascinated by studies of the occult—by meditation, mystical music, and studies of subjects such as astrology.

You are sensitive and sometimes baffling. Yet you are a most dynamic person. You have a strong sense of duty and always accomplish a lot in spite of yourself. Whatever you start gets finished, whether it is a homework assignment or a dull, dreary after-school job or chore.

Your assets are many. You are courageous and determined. You are also tender and sensitive to the inner needs of others. You have deep sympathy for and unswerving faith in people and in the ideas you believe in. No one has a greater sense of purpose than you, and no one will work harder toward a goal.

On the negative side, your main faults are selfishness and insecurity—and the two are related. When you are feeling positive about yourself, you are kind and thoughtful; but when you occasionally fall into the depths of Scorpio gloom, "I want" becomes your byword. You are rebellious and pick fights with those closest to you. Nothing and no one seem to please. You become contradictory and sharp tongued. If someone says "yes," you automatically say "no."

These negative moods happen because way down deep you are feeling pessimistic about yourself and about your future. Self-pity and self-doubt get a double hold, which you can best shake if you keep moving and concentrate on the bright side of things. For your basic nature is constructive, though feelings of doom and gloom do creep in occasionally and are part of your complicated temperament. For some reason, it is hard for you to value yourself as highly as others do. But such doubts are usually in your mind, rather than in the facts.

Whatever your feelings, they are earnest and strong. Whatever you feel, you feel with a burning intensity. And when you protest, you really mean it. Your temper rarely flares, but when it does, it is quick and forceful. Luckily, you get over anger just as quickly.

Bravery is another Scorpio characteristic. When anything sad or painful happens, you take it without flinching. And when you are ill or there is a sudden change of plans, you are a good sport.

As said before, your Scorpio personality contains many apparent contradictions. Your nature is intense and dramatic, but based on deep, abiding affection.

PHYSICAL CHARACTERISTICS

You have natural good health and an exceptionally strong body. You move with power and work with energy, and you rarely get ill. When you do, if the ailment is minor, you are likely to keep on your feet long after another would have gone to bed. In other words, you fight illness the way you do anything else—hard. You also recuperate more quickly than others. And you are brave and face pain far better than most.

The main danger to your health is of going at

things so hard you drain your energies. This may be emotional or physical, but it can be prevented by getting plenty of rest and eating well-balanced meals.

In appearance, Scorpios tend to be strong, sturdy types. More often than not, they have dark complexions and deep-set eyes.

Male Scorpios often have bushy eyebrows and a determined-looking jawline, while female Scorpios are likely to have oval faces and a special, mysterious sort of beauty. They look young all their lives and have a quiet but strong sex appeal.

Scorpio is a Water sign, and all Scorpios have a special feeling about the sea. Both sexes wear a lot of blue and white. Female Scorpios love pearls as accessories, while males may own mother-of-pearl cuff links.

The tones you prefer are deep, and you like clothes that are dramatic, and slightly daring. A Scorpio male always looks elegant, even in sports outfits, and a Scorpio female wears clothes exceptionally well. She has the intriguing kind of looks that men gravitate toward and other girls envy.

Just one caution: A Scorpio female probably should not wear yellow on dates. She is an extremely jealous type, and this color could bring out the green in her complexion, leading to a sallow look.

SCHOOL AND CAREER

You have more drive than any of the signs, and determination gets you far in school, as it does later in a career. Your only problem here may be one of temperament. Strong shifts of mood can affect the quality of your work, and you sometimes balk at authority, especially if you think a certain teacher is unfair or a certain subject is taught in an old-fashioned or foolish way. When this happens, you are likely to rebel and become contradictory.

Most of the time, however, you are systematic and capable and should make high marks. You always do your assignments and you almost never give up. You will go ahead and try to solve a problem even if you don't understand it. You have great powers of concentration, are also creative, and sometimes seem to be touched by a streak of genius.

Because Scorpios are so dynamic and resourceful, they invariably do well in their careers. As a Scorpio, you are able to handle any job and any emergency. You are quick-witted and lead with natural ease.

Scorpio males have a strong urge to explore, and add a dramatic flair to whatever they do. They make excellent doctors, lawyers, research scientists, detectives, and professors. They are enthusiastic about things of a mystical nature and may join a religious order or even become philosophers or astrologers. And because they have good money sense, investment banking and the stock market might be fields of interest.

Scorpio females are likely to do something creative. They have keen powers of observation and might work in personnel or as a critic. Or their love of investigation might lead them to writing or social work. Scorpio females who start as receptionists and secretaries are likely to climb to high positions of leadership. Acting and fashion modeling should also appeal to their dramatic natures.

MONEY

You work hard to earn the money you need. But you also have a so-called "golden touch" and are financially lucky.

This is fortunate, because yours is an extravagant sign. You like nice things and you like quality. Your achievements will be considerable, but so are your desires. You yearn for luxury more than most, and want the best, for yourself and others. You spend liberally and are also a generous giver. Your donation to a favorite charity or cause will always be on the large side. You are also excellent at managing and raising money, and may even be chairman of the fund.

You never pinch pennies or count the cost of the fun you are having, and anyone who splits a restaurant bill with you gets more than his fair share. On the other hand, you are good at systematic saving. You never hoard, but your Scorpio feeling for always keeping something hidden extends to your bank account. It would be unlike you to ever be completely broke.

FUN AND LEISURE

ALL Scorpios like strenuous sports and have a deep feeling about water sports. Male Scorpios are likely to go out for boxing and wrestling, as well as ice hockey, surfing, swimming, and sailing. Female Scorpios make graceful figure skaters and fast swimmers, and are among the best tennis players. Both combine strength and agility with good timing and a sense of daring.

Mysteries, science-fiction thrillers, and romantic novels are all favorite Scorpio reading. Record favorites often have religious overtones and lots of "soul." The love of mystery extends through Scorpio's favorite movies and plays, and a Scorpio always likes to see something that makes him or her feel strongly emotional. Drama—the more intense the better—is the meat of the Scorpio existence.

A Scorpio's party preference is for small "just us" gatherings rather than big blasts. Light chitchat is annoying to a Scorpio, who prefers intimate, deep discussions, or at least sharp, lively repartee. Yet Scorpios are charming, magnetic hosts and hostesses. They are among the few who give successful surprise parties. In fact, any party a Scorpio gives is likely to have some element of surprise about it—who comes next or what happens next.

Scorpios feel as intensely about travel as anything else, but they rarely travel just for fun's sake. Rather, they travel to accomplish something—to learn, to delve, or to do. Perhaps that is why so many Scorpios are found in study groups going to Europe, on modern-day music pilgrimages, and, later, in the Peace Corps.

HOME AND FAMILY

TEMPERAMENTALLY, Scorpios don't seem like homebodies, but home is very important to you. Your emotional nature, more than others, needs the comfort and reassurance of a well-ordered and stable home life.

You are proud of where you live and of your family. You are loving and loyal, and no one sticks up more strongly for other family members. But you are prone to moody spells, and you sometimes snap back at brothers and sisters or your parents. Your temper is quick, especially if your feelings are hurt or you think you haven't gotten your fair share.

On the other hand, you delight in keeping your own things orderly and gladly do regular duties as well as lend a hand with the lawn or the dishes.

You like to have company, but not all of the time. You must have some corner, some private and personal place to think your deep Scorpio thoughts. More than others, you are likely to keep a diary or scrapbook, and your own room may reflect several decorative themes.

You listen, and sympathetically, to anything your parents have to say. But sometimes, if their path is not yours, you become sullen and silent, which can build a small grievance into real resentment. At such a time you would do better to speak up, with tact and affectionate concern, plus the strength of your true convictions. Feeling misunderstood and sorry for yourself will only lead to worse scenes later. Keep showing the positive part of your Scorpio nature and your home relations will be even happier.

FRIENDSHIP

As a Scorpio, you have the capacity for deep, lasting friendship. But you must, if you are the fiery type of Scorpio, curb your temper and your tongue—and your tendency to tell other people what to do. Your seeming dominance is really only a cover-up for deep-seated feelings of insecurity, and your good friends know this. They know also that your temper is a bluff. Underneath you are frightened, and yearning for reassurance and affection.

Because there are so many contradictions to your Scorpio nature, you are likely to have only a few close friends who know you really well. They will be loyal and loving, and sympathetic to even your widest swings of emotion.

Because you are bright and witty, you also will have a number of casual friends and acquaintances. But you are not completely comfortable making light conversation with someone you have just met for the first time. You may even act flippant or moody, or in some way not seem your real self. For instance, what you mean in jest may sound sarcastic. That's why there are always one or two people who say they can't quite figure you out.

Your personality is baffling on the one hand and one of the most magnetic on the other.

People are drawn to you, and once you know a person well, you are capable of the closest and most meaningful kind of friendship.

ROMANCE

ALL Scorpios have strong, intense love natures. As a Scorpio, your feelings are highly emotional, and you have a deep-seated need to be loved and appreciated.

Scorpios do not flirt or tease or take love lightly. You are demonstrative (unless you are in that certain Scorpio mood to retreat and be mysterious and secretive). Also, you want and expect your love to be returned in full. Your nature is possessive and you are easily made jealous. A Scorpio male really doesn't like it when someone else dances with his date, and a Scorpio female is inwardly wild when her escort does a courtly favor for another girl.

But while you are capable of a deep dislike for anyone who comes between you and the object of your affections, you are also extremely loyal to the person you like. You praise the person warmly and will do anything to please. You are unusually attentive, and equally generous with compliments and single roses. And you are the most faithful of all types.

The Scorpio male is dynamic and masculine and extremely attractive to the opposite sex. He is unhappy unless he is loved, and he loves deeply. And when he gives his heart, he will go to any lengths to protect and care for the person he cares about. Usually he is interested in only one person at a time, for it would be unlike him to carry on several romances, or even flirtations, at once.

Therefore, the girl who dates a Scorpio male must be very careful not to make him jealous. She must avoid even the appearance of seeming fickle, because the Scorpio male is the most possessive and proud of all types.

The Scorpio male also needs a lot of praise and attention. He is basically strong, but still his ego needs shoring up. And he is shattered by criticism, or when he has a quarrel with "the" one.

The Scorpio female is equally intriguing and romantic. She is intense and emotional, and has an aura of mystery about her. She gives a great deal, but always holds a slight something back. And she is warmly demonstrative unless she has reason to be suspicious or unsure of herself. When this happens, she will likely withdraw or pick an argument, which her date should recognize as a signal that what she really wants is affectionate reassurance.

The Scorpio female is somewhat hard to figure out. Occasionally she is maddening. On the other hand, she is responsive and fascinating, and invariably faithful when she wants to be. Moreover, she has excellent intuition in her romantic choices. The Scorpio female, like the Scorpio male, is as lucky in love as in anything else.

COMPATIBILITY GUIDE

WITH ARIES: This should be an intense twosome. You are both energetic, dynamic types, and you are both likely to want to lead. But there is a strong basic attraction, and you can probably work out any differences if you think unselfishly and put yourself in your partner's place.

WITH TAURUS: Taurus and Scorpio both have strong personalities, but their characteristics are completely different. Taurus is a patient, quiet person. Scorpio is fiery and sometimes feisty. But with a great deal of loving effort, you may well be able to prove the point that opposites really do attract.

WITH GEMINI: Two restless individuals with varied interests may clash—or find a haven in each other's company. In a way, talkative and changeable Gemini is ideal at bringing Scorpio's hidden talents into the light. But there will be trouble if flighty Gemini arouses the strong Scorpio jealousy. Affection and understanding are equally important.

WITH CANCER: Yours should be a harmonious and successful relationship. You are both Water signs, full of feeling and natural empathy for each other. But because you both are so responsive, there may be constant hurt feelings. Also, you both tend to shove small difficulties aside—though it is important that they be discussed openly before they become big problems.

WITH LEO: You are likely to have a lot of differences of opinion—about people, about things you like, about what to do. And Scorpio may be too possessive for independent Leo. Your personalities are strong and your natures passionate. Whether you are compatible or clash depends on how much you really care for each other.

WITH VIRGO: You are drawn to each other because you are so different. Steady, practical Virgo helps to stabilize sensitive, secretive Scorpio. Also on the plus side, the warmer aspects of the Scorpio nature tend to relax Virgo's restraint. If you are both tolerant and patient, the relationship should be successful.

WITH LIBRA: Libra is ruled by the mind; Scorpio by the emotions—which means that it may be hard for you to establish a common ground. But Libra is so charming and has such a talent for getting along with people that anything can happen—especially when the other person involved is a fascinating Scorpio!

WITH SCORPIO: You may irritate each other—or the attraction may be doubly magnetic. Even then, there are likely to be problems, for you both will be intensely jealous of each other. Success or failure depends on whether you pull together or pull each other apart.

WITH SAGITTARIUS: Sagittarius likes to be free, while Scorpio wants to possess. Sagittarius has a light-hearted sense of fun, whereas Scorpio is sensitive and serious. What happens here depends on how much real affection you have for each other, and how much you are each willing to adjust.

WITH CAPRICORN: Scorpio is expert at bringing out all the warm, loving qualities in the sometimes stern Capricorn nature. On the other hand, Capricorn knows just what to do to shake sensitive, sometimes oversensitive Scorpio out of a bad mood. This relationship is usually more than the sum of its parts.

WITH AQUARIUS: Independent Aquarius shies away from possessive Scorpio. The result is likely to be indifference. But if Scorpio is determined, and Aquarius is an affectionate type, your relationship could develop into a delightful companionship—with the promise, perhaps, of more.

WITH PISCES: You are both romantic and possessive and should be perfect partners. Any jealousy would be regarded as loving protection rather than a cause of problems. But sharp-tongued Scorpio should be careful not to hurt dreamy, idealistic Pisces' feelings. However, romantic Pisces does love to kiss and make up, so any differences should easily be resolved.

SAGITTARIUS

★ *November 23 - December 20* ★

ELEMENT: *Fire*
RULED BY: *Jupiter*
SYMBOL: *Archer*
KEY WORD: *Outgoing*
JEWEL: *Amethyst*
COLORS: *Purple, Red, Yellow, Blue;*
Rich Colors
LUCKY NUMBER: *3*
LUCKY DAY: *Thursday*

OTHER IMPORTANT SAGITTARIANS:
Sammy Davis, Jr.
Maria Callas
William F. Buckley, Jr.
Robert Goulet
Julie Harris
Paul Klee
Margaret Mead
Mary Martin
James Thurber
Frank Sinatra
Jane Fonda
John Lindsay
Mark Twain
Ludwig van Beethoven

SAGITTARIUS

GENERAL CHARACTERISTICS

You are outgoing and active, and people are instinctively drawn to you. Perhaps that's because of your innate courtesy, and the fact that you care so deeply about others. Or it could be because you are an interesting and good-humored person to know. It could also be because of your intelligence, which is creative and keen, and full of the kind of searching curiosity that "wants to know."

Your joy of living is tremendous. You are also an idealist. You look for the good in everyone and would rather be considered gullible than suspicious. You hate "hard" facts, which occasionally causes you problems in school. You set out to change the world, and frequently do.

Your life style is spontaneous rather than well thought out; your aim is happiness not security; your pace is swift instead of deliberate.

You are responsive to joy—in others, in nature, and in what you are doing. Only from time to time do you have darker moods, caused by the clash of what you are with what you want to be.

Also, because you are a Fire sign, you tend to dramatize everything. Once in a while you even create problems for yourself. That is why, more than others, you need warm, sympathetic friends and a family that will understand and guide you without seeming to push. You do not like being told what to do and can take criticism only if it is dished out with love and tact. Though you have a quick smile and ready sense of humor, you are not as easygoing as you seem.

But your complex temperament only makes you a more intriguing person to know. You are so many things at once: fair most of the time but petty when you feel cornered; full of vitality most of the time yet lazy when you are not really enthusiastic about something; idealistic about major aims and ideals but inconsiderate about being on time.

You have a great sense of fun. Occasionally it is hard to know whether you are teasing or being serious, and you have an uncanny knack for takeoffs and parody. Your repartee is swift, and always hits the nail on the head.

Your interests are as varied as your talents. You are vital and always on the go. But you will do best in the long run if you learn not to scatter your energies over too wide a field.

PHYSICAL CHARACTERISTICS

You have great vitality, more than any other sign. You also have a well-developed body and generally good health. Wearing yourself out through too much activity and an occasional tendency to live on your nerves are the only dangers to lasting good health. And you are sometimes careless about the basic rules: eating a balanced diet, getting enough rest, and taking any prescribed medicine.

But you never forget to get enough exercise. You are an out-of-doors person and don't feel really well unless you have taken a brisk walk or bike ride or done something invigorating with your body.

Physically, you are likely to be on the tall side. You are an athletic type with confident good looks. You are unusually graceful, have excellent posture, a clear skin, and generally vivid coloring.

In clothes, Sagittarians of both sexes like bright colors, rich materials, and random patterns (curves, and birds and flowers, rather than plaids or small geometric patterns).

You like extravagant clothes, especially slacks and jackets for Sagittarian males and pants suits and beach shifts for Sagittarian females. Any wardrobe problem is likely to be in the area of coordination, for you are prone to impulse purchases. And sometimes your bargains are not what you really need, or are not well-made. You would also do well to pay a little closer attention to your grooming. It is easy for you to forget a needed haircut or visit to the dentist. And Sagittarian females in a hurry sometimes put make-up on in a too haphazard way.

On the other hand, you have an intuitively good eye for what looks well on you. You dress with flair and dash, and never go unnoticed.

SCHOOL AND CAREER

You have an abundant supply of mental energy and a vivid, creative imagination. You do exceptionally well in school as long as you are really interested. If you lose interest—and usually this happens when you think a subject is boring or the method of teaching is not sufficiently stimulating—you may appear lazy, or develop an unfortunate "I don't care" attitude.

You show an especially strong aptitude for the arts, and love to be in dramatic productions and on debating teams. You thoroughly enjoy lively off-the-cuff class discussion, and are quick-witted and spontaneous when called on to recite.

Your scholastic snag lies in organization. You hate to outline and plan ahead. Long term papers generally "throw" you, and you have trouble keeping on a schedule. No matter how much time you have, you end up doing everything at the last minute. Still, you have an uncanny knack for getting good grades. In fact, you frequently do far better than the so-called grinds. Your method may be a bit haphazard, but your intuition and imagination rarely let you down.

And when you choose a career, your intuition and long-range judgment are equally excellent. It's only the short-range results that are, at times, ineffective. You may accept a job too quickly, or you may "throw in the towel" when your surroundings seem uninspired or the people you work for dull. And if your superiors are practical, stick-in-the-mud types, you will definitely clash. Or you may feel that you are being held back creatively. In such a case, it is best to make a change—but not rashly, or before you have thought out the next move.

Many careers are suited to your special Sagittarian nature. Anything with a touch of idealism is a natural. You might be a minister, or in the Peace Corps, or be part of a reform movement. Anything to do with travel or foreign countries would appeal.

Sagittarian males are drawn toward the construction business, teaching, and journalism.

Sagittarian females gravitate toward promotion, and active "girl Friday" jobs. And many of both sexes are found in acting, advertising, and real estate. Whatever you do, your outlook is slightly visionary and you want plenty of freedom to do your own thing—which you invariably do uniquely and well.

MONEY

YOU are anything but penny-wise. Your nature is extravagant and your financial instincts are impulsive—and you too often have to borrow because you have gotten into a financial hole of your own making. Still, and in spite of momentary problems, you are usually well off, and you have an unusual number of lucky breaks.

Wealth in the pocket is not one of your life aims. You are happy-go-lucky, and instinctively hate to save or think about security. Perhaps you succeed in this department of life because you are not uptight about it. You take more chances than more cautious signs. And while the dangers are greater, so are the rewards.

Whatever you earn is through your own efforts, for you are fiercely opposed to financial aid. You would far rather earn the money for something than have it given to you. With your nose for good fortune, you almost always—and without planning—achieve money as well as your real goal, happiness.

FUN AND LEISURE

You love the out of doors and nature more than any other sign. You thrive on competitive sports and do well in them, but you enjoy even more the solitary pleasures of a ride on a galloping horse, a brisk walk in the woods, a fast schuss down a slightly dangerous ski slope, or ice skating at full speed. You also love water sports, especially sailing. In all, your preference is for the dramatic and the adventurous.

As a Sagittarian, you have a strongly philosophical bent. You like "think" books, and can argue the pros and cons of anything. And you are drawn to anything with a touch of mystery about it. Suspense stories delight you. So does music that to others might seem strange and "other worldly."

Sagittarians are natural party-givers. You like to mix all kinds of people, and it almost always works. Your gatherings are lively and casual, yet there are likely to be more deep discussions than light chitchat. (You can't stand shallow people or meaningless chatter.)

Entertainment will be spontaneous with you. Any party at your place is bound to be a happening of the best and most delightful sort.

You are a Fire sign, which means you like to be on the move. You are a born traveler, and a good one. There isn't a country or a community you wouldn't like to explore.

And wherever you go, you will avoid the cliche choice and the beaten tourist path. Your approach is creative and personal, and you invariably have twice the trip that others do.

HOME AND FAMILY

You are not as domestic as some of the signs, and you are away from your home more than others. But you like, and need, to have roots. You always want to return to home base, and you are deeply attached to your family.

Because of your natural charm and adaptability, you usually get along very well with other family members—brothers, sisters, and parents. Any serious break between you is rare. The only problem is that you sometimes get the blues and feel misunderstood. You may resent being told anything, and get a slight chip on your shoulder about what you consider to be somewhat stodgy and behind the times in your parents' idea of what is good for you. What you want is indulgence, and what you are likely to get is wholesome, constructive encouragement. Luckily, your moods do not last long, and your family's firm, gentle guidance helps restore you to Sagittarian harmony.

Because you are creative, your home—and your room—are likely to have unusual and artistic touches. Your taste is excellent. And while your room may not be tidy, it is individualistic. It is likely to contain strong colors, and evidence —collections, banners, and bulletin boards—of your many outside interests.

FRIENDSHIP

YOUR vitality, basic optimism, and good humor draw others to you like a magnet. You have many friends, and you rarely lose a friend.

Communication is your meat. You want to discuss, probe, analyze, and share. You want to air your feelings and find out how other people feel and think. And you are exceptionally helpful and sympathetic to any friend in trouble. (You are also sympathetic to all causes and minority groups, especially when anyone is taken advantage of or is considered the underdog.)

The only time your high ideals get you into difficulty is when you put a friend on too high a pedestal. When that person falls off, and does anything rude or inconsiderate, you are deeply disillusioned—sometimes out of proportion to the incident.

But most of the time your good nature tempers your inner sensitivity. And your ability to laugh at yourself helps you retain a sense of proportion.

You are as many-sided in friendship as in other aspects of your life. Your friends are from different neighborhoods and have different life styles. And you genuinely enjoy them all. This open-mindedness, plus your sense of consideration and your ability to really listen, makes you one of the most popular of any of the signs.

ROMANCE

SAGITTARIANS are never wallflowers in the romantic department. Members of both sexes have many admirers—often at once.

Your nature is sympathetic and affectionate. Yet you love your freedom. Maybe that's why you make so many impulsive attachments—and then end them before they become serious. Your feelings are positive and sincere at the time. It's just that your feelings tend to wander. And no one can tie you down against your will.

You completely charm the opposite sex by your thoughtfulness and spontaneity. You know how to delight with the unexpected gift, the spur-of-the-moment gesture. The person you are with always feels very special. You also remember the little personal details about him or her. And you are the type to give one flower, or a particularly amusing and meaningful card or book, rather than a more showy but less thoughtful gift.

On the other hand, the person you are interested in never quite knows when you are going to call, or what you are going to do. This unpredictable quality is part of your attraction—though it can be annoying at times.

You are exceptionally generous and honest. Someone to care about definitely brings out the best in your Sagittarian nature, and you shouldn't worry if you seem to care about a number of people. Eventually you will find just the right person, the one who most completely measures up to your ideals. Then your devotion and interest will be steady. Yet you will be as adventurous and romantic as ever. It's just that then there will be only one object of your affection instead of many.

The Sagittarian male makes a girl know she is a girl. He is a delightful companion and a real wit. He wants to share everything with his date—as well as have her sympathize a little with him. He is also a bit unconventional, and prefers a date who thinks for herself and doesn't necessarily follow the crowd—but does, of course, follow him.

The Sagittarian female is a complete idealist in love. She is romantic rather than practical, and is led entirely by her feelings. Who or what you are or what others say—she doesn't give a whit about these things. Her emotions are intuitive, impulsive, and sure—until she changes her mind.

She is exciting, slightly fiery, and hard to pin down. And a calculating approach turns her off. The Sagittarian female is her own person and values her freedom—at least until someone she deeply cares for (and there is usually just one lifetime love) convinces her otherwise.

COMPATIBILITY GUIDE

WITH ARIES: You are both Fire signs, and are strongly attracted to each other. The relationship should be creative and stimulating—as long as you don't lose your tempers at the same time. Think twice before you speak, and you should be able to work out any problems.

WITH TAURUS: Your life styles are entirely different. Sagittarius moves quickly and impulsively, whereas Taurus is a planner and goes slowly, one step at a time. What the two of you have in common is high ideals—a feeling that the world can be a better place because of you. And often it is.

WITH GEMINI: Gemini is flighty and somewhat of a flirt. Sagittarius is completely honest in love and never plays games. Your relationship should certainly be lively. Whether it works out in the long run depends on how much you each are willing to adjust, and on how deeply you really care.

WITH CANCER: Both of you like variety and are sensitive types, capable of enjoying life thoroughly. In spite of Cancer's moodiness, the two of you should be able to make beautiful music and have many happy times.

WITH LEO: Two Fire signs attract and stimulate each other. You both get the same kicks out of life, and anything you do is twice as much fun when you do it together. But it will take maturity to decide which of you is boss, for you are both born leaders. You may have some fiery times, but, above all, you should have fun.

WITH VIRGO: Virgo knows how to temper some of the natural Sagittarian impulsiveness. On the other hand, Sagittarius brings out the latent fun-loving qualities of more serious Virgo. You each fire the other to untapped depths, and should have a rewarding and rich relationship.

WITH LIBRA: You are each generous types, moved by the idealistic and beautiful. You both appreciate life and want to please. You are likely to have many friends, hopes, and desires in common. The only problem is that Sagittarius' impulsiveness and lack of long-term goals may irritate security-minded Libra. With any effort at all, the odds favor success.

WITH SCORPIO: You are both intrigued by the mystic and the mysterious, and you may be dealing with illusion rather than reality. The sooner you realize this, the sooner you can work toward the real potential of your relationship. Sagittarius is outgoing and good for secretive Scorpio. The attraction is definite, and you are likely to start off strong. Whether anything lasting comes of it depends on how mature you both are.

WITH SAGITTARIUS: This should be an exciting, dynamic relationship. Since you are both open-minded, you should be receptive to each other's feelings and views. On the other hand, you may expect too much of each other. You may expect perfection, which is impossible. Relax, and keep the lines of communication open, and much shared happiness should be yours.

WITH CAPRICORN: You should go well and far together. Capricorn is likely to spur Sagittarius on to heights he or she never dreamed of. On the other side of the coin, Sagittarius is best able to melt Capricorn's outer shell of reserve, releasing all the natural gaiety of that sign. You may both have to overlook small differences, but the rewards of real togetherness should make it well worth the effort.

WITH AQUARIUS: You not only care for each other but for the whole world. In other words, you accent each other's humanitarian impulses as well as light each other's personal fires. But judgment and planning are needed unless you are to fritter away your combined energies. Think carefully before you take any plunge.

WITH PISCES: The outlook is positive. You are both emotional and sensitive signs, though Sagittarius has a far stronger feeling of independence, while Pisces needs someone to lean on. Pisces' possessiveness is the poison that could mar this potentially great relationship.

CAPRICORN

★ *December 21 - January 19* ★

ELEMENT: *Earth*
RULED BY: *Saturn*
SYMBOL: *Mountain Goat*
KEY WORD: *Ambitious*
JEWEL: *Moonstone*
COLORS: *Green, Brown, White, Gray;*
Muted Tones
LUCKY NUMBER: 8
LUCKY DAY: *Saturday*

OTHER FAMOUS CAPRICORNIANS:
Joan Baez
Ray Bolger
Martin Luther King, Jr.
Richard M. Nixon
Danny Thomas
J. Edgar Hoover
Humphrey Bogart
Mao Tse-tung
Renata Tebaldi
Sandy Koufax
Marlene Dietrich
Cab Calloway
Pablo Casals
Ethel Merman

CAPRICORN

GENERAL CHARACTERISTICS

YOUR aim is to be at the top—in love, in school, and in whatever you do. You set high goals for yourself and almost always achieve them.

Like the Mountain Goat, the symbol of your sign, you climb ever upward. Others may move quickly, in impulsive spurts. Yours is a slow and steady pace. Small pitfalls along the way rarely cause you to stray from your path.

Sometimes you seem to be a real loner, again like the Mountain Goat high on his lofty peak. But such an impression misjudges your inner nature, which is warm and responsive, and aching for close contact with others. Buried beneath your more serious public face is a sense of humor that is light and almost frivolous.

You are the type about whom others say, "It takes a while to get to know him (or her)." Your real spontaneity and show off affection come to the fore only when you feel confident with another, and therefore free to show your true colors. This duality, of warmth and shyness, gives you a special charm, and your appeal is stronger for not being blatant.

Other characteristics of you as a Capricornian are ambition (your driving force), diplomacy, unswerving loyalty, and thrift. You have a fine mind and a wish to excel in whatever you do. And you inspire confidence in others. They profit by your willpower and by your courageous approach to anything you tackle. It is hard to think of a Capricorn giving up—ever!

You are reliable and can always be counted upon. You are somewhat conservative, but never narrow or straight-laced. On you, even the most avant-garde ideas and fads seem somehow sensible and appropriate.

Because your thinking is rarely muddled, you come right to the point in conversation. Others enjoy talking with you, especially when you let loose a little and your sense of humor shows.

You are not as moody as some other signs. Occasionally you feel inadequate because you have set such high standards that even *you* can't keep up. But you soon regain your sense of proportion and are rarely depressed for long.

You are one of the most thoughtful signs. And you live by the rule that actions speak louder than words. You never boast about what you are going to do for a friend, but simply sense the need and go out and do it.

You are modest in expecting thanks. But in the end you always receive the loyalty—and thanks—you deserve. And the good deeds you do are usually returned.

PHYSICAL CHARACTERISTICS

Your constitution is generally strong, and you have great powers of endurance. You throw most illness off before it takes hold, and rarely catch the colds and flu bugs that are making the rounds.

When you are ill, you want to get well fast. You are an excellent, well-disciplined patient. You don't try to buck the doctor's orders or forget to take your medicine.

Capricorn rules the joints and knees. When you fall skiing, you are most likely to twist your knee, and after a spurt of exercise, you may suffer from a charley horse. People born under your sign are also prone to occasional teeth and skin troubles. So take prompt care of any complexion and dental problems.

Capricornians are generally tall, and are usually slender. Problems crop up only when their love of good food gets in the way of a sensible diet. Luckily, Capricorn people have more willpower than most.

Your features are regular and you have exceptionally expressive eyes. At times you may look a little pale (which Capricorn males can correct by plenty of fresh air and exercise, and Capricorn females by using a blusher).

Capricornians of both sexes are the sort about whom others say, "Who is that person who just walked by?" You turn heads not only because of your basic good looks, but because of the total way you look and the appealing want-to-get-to-know-you-better impression you give.

This is partly because of the way you dress. You have excellent clothes sense and make the most of your wardrobe. Your style is conservative, but with a dash. A Capricorn male will wear a bright mod necktie with a traditional suit, while a Capricorn female will add colorful and unusual accessories—a belt, a string of beads, or a scarf—to her outfit. Your smile and the way you step out with confidence add a final touch to the good impression you give.

SCHOOL AND CAREER

You do well in school for a number of reasons. You are naturally bright and think in a clear, logical way.

And you are not so easily distracted as some other signs. When you are given an assignment, you stick to it until the work is finished. And when you read a book, you read it completely and carefully. You also know how to take good notes.

You have many outside interests, but are adept at handling a number of activities at once. It is almost unthinkable for you to loaf. And the only time you become disorganized is when you are under pressure—overnight papers and timed quizzes are apt to throw you out of kilter.

You prefer a well-planned pattern, and to work steadily rather than in spurts. Finally, you have great powers of concentration and can work even in noisy rooms and with the radio going. You have a special affinity for math and science, both of which appeal to your sense of order.

People born under the sign of Capricorn are ambitious and successful. They almost always reach their goals—though it may be later in life than for some other signs.

In other words, yours is never a flash-in-the-pan success. Nor are you likely to start out strong, as a boy or girl wonder, and then lose out in the long run. More likely your climb is upward, step by steady step, till you reach the top of your field.

You are a natural diplomat, and so are suited to politics and foreign service. You are also a careful craftsman. You might be a builder or a practical scientist, or do medical research. Social service and nature also interest you.

A Capricorn male might choose a career as a marine biologist or ecologist, or work in any field concerning math or money.

Capricorn females incline toward culture and the arts. They are frequently found in home service fields and in museums or agencies. They make excellent editors or supervisors of any kind, and are gifted, creative consultants in beauty or decoration.

MONEY

You like nice things and the security that money can bring. But you would far rather save up for something than go in debt. (If you ever do, you promptly pay back anything you owe.)

You want to have enough money—not for its own sake, but for the feeling of security it can bring. Being on the financial fringe makes you feel uncomfortable.

You are also thrifty. Christmas clubs and savings accounts appeal to you. You like to have something put aside, and you are a good credit risk throughout life.

You are not a natural gambler, and you are never wasteful.

You are more likely to plan your purchases and buy good things rather than splurge on fancy spur-of-the-moment purchases. On the other hand, you are not a penny-pincher, and you will help any friend in a tight spot. You love to give generous gifts and to make other people happy. Your reserves allow you to be giving, which is one of the best reasons for having them.

FUN AND LEISURE

IN sports, your tastes run to rather rugged individualistic sports. You combine a sense of daring with a great regard for safety, and rarely take chances or go too fast.

The sports you have the greatest affinity for are skiing, mountain climbing, scuba diving, surfing, hiking, and any kind of exploration. You are interested in these activities even if you don't have the time or opportunity to personally engage in them.

In books, you gravitate toward novels and the classics. And the records you play most frequently are likely to be old favorites. You may be a jazz buff.

Anything old has a special fascination for you. You might collect antiques or be interested in old cars. And you enjoy movies based on historical fact.

Most of the time you would rather be with one or two good friends than with a crowd. So you prefer to entertain in small groups. You feel somewhat swallowed up by a noisy, overcrowded party. The frivolous in you comes out in intimate gatherings where you can let go and be yourself. (You tell jokes well and are an excellent mimic.) Picnics and cookouts are among your favorite parties.

You love to travel, but don't like to have to rush. You would rather take in one town or resort at length than hurry from place to place and only hit the high points. But you are a thoughtful traveler and well remember where you have been and what you have seen. Nor do you mind going places alone, for you always seem to make friends along the way.

HOME AND FAMILY

You have a great sense of contentment at home and are close to your family. Friction is rare, and outbursts of anger somewhat frighten you.

You have the ability to talk problems out rather than let them grow. And you are generally looked up to by younger brothers and sisters, who ask your advice and look to you for an example.

You are also helpful around the house. You know the value of getting any nasty chores over with so you can go on to what is fun.

Sometimes, however, you are moody and may brood. This happens whenever you feel slighted for any reason. Activity and your own sense of proportion usually bring back your good spirits before depression gets too strong a hold on you. You rarely feel really depressed or sorry for yourself.

You are always bent on some sort of self-improvement. You like to be tidy, and are generally engaged in projects around the house. You are well-organized, and if you say you will do twenty push-ups each morning or clean out a closet, you do it.

Because you are so self-contained, you rarely clash with your parents. Yet you need their love and approval and suffer greatly when there is any disagreement.

Luckily, you are unusually mature and they are understanding. Any problems are usually worked out smoothly and quickly. Your contribution to a happy home life is great—and so is the return it brings to you.

FRIENDSHIP

You don't make friends quite as quickly as some signs, but the friends you make you keep, often for life.

And your best friends are deeply loyal and close to you. That's partly because with them you let go of your Capricorn reserve and shed that dignified cloak you sometimes wear with strangers.

You never mean to keep people at a distance, but you do feel awkward when you are not sure of another person's reactions—as on a blind date or in a different group.

You value your friends highly. You can always be counted on to help them in any way. You never tell their secrets or make cutting remarks. And you let them have the limelight. Your own self-confidence is so strong that you don't have to toot your own horn. Yet because you are modest and unassuming you receive more than your share of compliments and you are popular.

You also have a strong sense of privacy and a need to be by yourself from time to time. You well know the difference between being lonely and being alone.

When you are refreshed, you rejoin your friends, and are ready for a round of fun and good conversation—and to do all the things that two can do better than one.

ROMANCE

IN romance, you blow warm or cold depending on how you feel about someone—whether you like him or her a little or a lot—and on how long you have known each other. Generally, it takes a fair amount of time for you to develop a relationship. You rarely fall in love at first sight. And you never commit yourself until you are sure of your own feelings. (Then you not only say how you feel, but are delightfully creative about expressing it.)

Dating just one person can become a drag when you are not really interested, so you are most likely to play the field, or even give love a temporary second place to your many other interests.

Yet love is essential to your happiness—and to bring out the warm inner you. So you are not likely to act the part of a lone wolf for long.

184

You hardly ever flirt (it doesn't seem sincere to you) and you don't think it a bit funny when someone *you* like flirts. When this happens, you withdraw or become jealous. And you kid no one by saying "It doesn't matter." It does—terribly.

That's because idealism is a basic part of your romantic nature. You feel strongly, though sometimes not too realistically. And you find it impossible to compromise or to pretend to anything you don't feel from the bottom of your heart.

Eventually, when you fall in love, it is likely to be forever. You will give each other the attention and affection you both need and want—and you will be one of the most demonstrative of signs.

Until that time, you may seem fickle and a little hard to get—which only intrigues others and eggs them on. You are a delightful date in every way. You not only attract, you also present quite a challenge.

Capricorn males need lots of encouragement in romantic matters. Sometimes they are shy and let the romantic offensive slide—but they are eager to please and will be delighted to be invited somewhere by a more aggressive female. Capricorn males are this way because they are really afraid of being rebuffed or turned down—which is ridiculous, because they are charming, considerate, and quite exceptionally enjoyable people.

One warning: while slow to get to know a person, a Capricorn male will sometimes end a relationship abruptly and without warning. When his feelings change, he is too sincere to keep on dating that person. But if his feeling is sure, it will never change.

The same steadfast quality in romance is true of the Capricorn female—but only after she has made up her mind that this person is "the" one. And this usually takes her a long time compared to other signs. But then she is exceptionally responsive and warm-hearted.

Until then, she may want to date a lot of people and may be a good companion more than anything else. Frequently, the companionship grows into love. If not, she will be sincere in saying how she feels. It may take her a long time to find the person she is looking for, but she almost always does, and is capable of achieving great happiness in togetherness.

COMPATIBILITY GUIDE

WITH ARIES: Success depends on how much real giving there is in the relationship. Aries must avoid a domineering attitude, but the Aries energy and zest should spur thoughtful Capricorn on to great heights. And Capricorn will temper Aries' impulsiveness. You should both benefit from this association.

WITH TAURUS: This relationship may simply not get off the ground, because both of you are waiting for the other to make a move. But if it does, you will have the rare kind of togetherness that comes from much in common, plus feeling the same way emotionally.

WITH GEMINI: Flighty Gemini is likely to fascinate more serious Capricorn. But Gemini must be careful not to go too far in teasing or flirting. Capricorn doesn't care for games, and is likely to end the relationship abruptly—cutting off the possibilities of a really delightful twosome.

WITH CANCER: You are drawn toward each other as the sea toward the moon. This strong personal magnetism is likely to outweigh any minor differences of opinion and some dissimilarity in tastes. And Capricorn gives the oversensitive Cancer a much needed feeling of self-confidence.

WITH LEO: Harmony will result only if Leo curbs his or her desire to lead. Leo should make a special effort to listen to Capricorn, who may withdraw. Communication is the key word here. Patience and effort should result in delightful togetherness and a relationship with many shared interests.

WITH VIRGO: You are well suited to each other. Few adjustments should be needed to make this a smooth relationship—in fact, there is a slight danger of it being *too* smooth, and of your eventually becoming bored with each other. The important thing is never to take each other for granted.

WITH LIBRA: There is a strong and naturally sympathetic bond between you. Jealousy on either side could cause a separation. But you know how to jog each other out of any bad moods, and you are on the same wave length. The harmony in this relationship should be very close.

WITH SCORPIO: Scorpio may be a little too intense for more restrained Capricorn. Yet you fire each other's energies and you are both strongly drawn to the romantic and mystic. You are genuine soul mates, and your communication is a special kind of personal shorthand.

WITH SAGITTARIUS: You complement each other nicely. Sagittarius is outgoing and high-spirited; Capricorn tends to be reserved and quiet. Yet your secret desires incline toward the opposite traits. People may wonder what you see in each other. They find it hard to believe how really compatible the two of you are. You have many surface variations in taste, but few deep or serious differences.

WITH CAPRICORN: The fact that you are so alike also means that you have the same faults. You may bicker more than other couples, or you may both retreat at the same time—getting you and the relationship nowhere. Still and all, the attraction is strong and you have a lot going for you. Caring is what counts.

WITH AQUARIUS: You are both driven by high ideals and a feeling that you will somehow change the world. And together the possibilities are twice as strong! But you must openly discuss any differences before they lead to a real breach. And Capricorn must never make free-dom-loving Aquarius feel that he or she is being hemmed in.

WITH PISCES: Pisces is so openly affectionate that Capricorn will find his or her charm hard to resist. You are both considerate and will be able to sympathize with each other's problems. Additionally, each of you craves peace and emotional security—which you will find, most likely, together.

AQUARIUS

★ *January 20 - February 18* ★

ELEMENT: *Air*
RULED BY: *Uranus*
SYMBOL: *Water Bearer*
KEY WORD: *Humanitarian*
JEWEL: *Sapphire*
COLORS: *Lavender, Yellow-Green, Red, Blue;*
Off-Beat Shades
LUCKY NUMBER: *4*
LUCKY DAY: *Saturday*

OTHER IMPORTANT AQUARIANS:
Mia Farrow
Paul Newman
Charles Darwin
Charles Lindbergh
Norman Mailer
James Dean
Vanessa Redgrave
Eartha Kitt
Gypsy Rose Lee
U Thant
Leontyne Price
Franklin D. Roosevelt
Thomas Edison
W. Somerset Maugham

AQUARIUS

GENERAL CHARACTERISTICS

You combine the visionary and the practical. Your love of humanity is one of your outstanding characteristics. You not only feel strongly, but you set out to change ways you consider narrow or ill-advised—and frequently you do.

You are also an innovator, a real pioneer. You are always way ahead of other signs in new thoughts and original approaches to old problems. Anything you do, from cooking to woodworking, benefits from your creative flair.

You never follow sheep-like. You wear what you wish and pick friends because you like them, and you stand up for your beliefs even if they are unpopular. Sometimes you seem a little unconventional, and even in the spirit of your protest, you never quite follow the crowd.

You are always fair and tolerant. And you prefer people who aren't "just like you." Certainly you are one of the most completely multi-dimensional of the signs; intellectual yet emotional, fond of tradition yet an innovator, devoted to peace yet an energetic, strong-willed worker.

Moreover, you value personal freedom highly. You can be led (if it is done gently and affectionately), but you can never be driven, and you resent authority when it seems demanding or harsh. People can't quite pin you down and you sometimes resent their trying.

But they can be sure of your basic kindness and consideration. You believe in and live by the ideal of the brotherhood of man. Very occasionally Aquarians neglect those personally close to them in the pursuit of general ideals. But most of the time, Aquarians successfully combine the abstract and the intimate.

Frequently, the first impression of an Aquarian is that he or she is rather detached and "hard to get to know." This may be true. For an Aquarian has to know you fairly well before revealing his or her deep feeling and emotions.

You also seem this way because you are somewhat shy about showing all your colors until you know how the other person feels. You may act gay and amusing, but are not being quite yourself. In addition, you have a very real sense of personal privacy. You hate gossip, and you respect secrets and intimate feelings—your own and others.

Aquarian pitfalls are that sometimes you are too much of a dreamer, and you frequently find it hard to take criticism. And while you love to be creative, practical details like cleaning up bore you. But all the snags are minor and can be ironed out by a little Aquarian effort and will-power.

PHYSICAL CHARACTERISTICS

You are stronger than you seem. In spite of a build likely to be on the slight side, you have an abundance of energy and rarely get sick. (And when you do, you hate to admit it.)

But you do at times feel intimidated by others, or opposed by what you feel to be unfair criticism. And sometimes this affects your nerves. You may have mild headaches or an upset stomach. This is less likely to happen if you avoid too much pressure and speak up when you are angry rather than hold it back.

Also, it is important that you keep fairly regular hours and have a good, balanced diet.

Aquarian males have a kind of rugged, he-man good looks. They have a special look of mystery, and are the sort seen in spy movies.

Aquarian females have a fascination all their own. They have winning smiles, and their eyes are usually their outstanding feature. They are imaginative but never overpowering in the use of make-up, and are likely to wear their hair a number of different ways.

In dress, Aquarians of both sexes are pace-setters. They develop new styles and set the trends others follow. A few overdo the kooky look, but most Aquarians combine traditional, basic clothes with creative, mod accessories. And they save anything really far-out for home and leisure wear.

In color, purple, yellow-green, red, and white are the Aquarian weaknesses. They also like rich fabrics, plaids, and anything that's a bargain.

SCHOOL AND CAREER

You are an idea person, even at school. Your agile mind darts and skips about, and sees associations others miss. You are excellent in all creative work and are inventive in finding the shortest path to a finished assignment.

You are a willing student and enjoy hard work—as long as it is stimulating. But you are not a plodder, and your concentration is on the total picture—and on relationships—rather than on amassing or memorizing facts. (You never can seem to remember historical dates, and the discipline and exactness of math makes this subject difficult for you.)

Your desk is likely to be cluttered, and you never outline anything if you can help it.

Others think you disorganized, but this is not so. It's just that your organization is inner and intuitive. Your mind is always working, usually along new paths.

Scholastic freedom—the right to speak up— means a lot to you. And you will protest anyone or anything that infringes on this freedom. But you do it eloquently and without malice.

Your sign has produced more geniuses and more pioneers than any other. Aquarian students may not top the honor roll, but they invariably show creative ability and the promise of great things to come.

Whatever career you choose should be stimulating, and you will invariably give it your own individual slant.

You are an energetic worker and can accomplish a job in half the time it takes another. But routine bores you. You prefer a job that is varied and not too rigidly supervised.

Both male and female Aquarians have a special fondness for the arts. They make fine writers, artists, actors, and actresses. And Acquarians are the best suited of all the signs for social work. Helping others appeals to them.

The pioneering instinct of male Aquarians may lead them into becoming engineers, inventors, designers, or archaeologists. Results and self-development are the male Aquarian's career aims. But in spite of his non-commercial attitude, he is usually outstandingly successful financially.

Female Aquarians are frequently teachers (especially in progressive schools), advertising whizzes, travel agents, or television personalities. They often prefer work on a freelance basis, as authors, editors, graphic designers or illustrators, and most often combine their work with an equally creative and fulfilling domestic life.

MONEY

AQUARIANS never set out to make money, but they usually do. That's because they work hard, and with the kind of creative efficiency that cuts time and gets results.

The Aquarian isn't extravagant, but he or she is impulsive. An Aquarian is likely to skimp on necessities and splurge on something he or she personally likes—a new record album or an impractical but pretty dress.

Budgets are alien to the Aquarian nature. So

is saving. But since you eventually learn that money worries drain your energy, you may begrudgingly put something aside for a rainy day.

Because money is a means to an end, rather than a goal, you are poor at investing and at bargaining. The rate you set for baby-sitting or mowing someone's lawn tends to be too low, and later in life you are likely to make poorly thought-out purchases of penny stocks rather than put your money in solid blue chips.

But somehow, and in spite of yourself, you are as lucky concerning money as you are generous in sharing what you have with others.

FUN AND LEISURE

AQUARIANS love nature and the out-of-doors, but they are not particularly big at team sports. Their preferences run to individual water sports, horseback riding, hiking, and tennis. (They are fast on their feet and play a good game based on speed and the unexpected move.)

Hobbies are important to Aquarians, and they frequently feel starved for a good book or magazine article. But they also enjoy the company of others in pastimes such as bowling, cards, and belonging to clubs or societies. Sometimes the aim is idealistic, and other times the group gathers just for fun.

The Aquarian loves parties—and the more colorful the better. Eccentric, off-beat people intrigue him or her, though an Aquarian feels equally at home in conservative circles. That's because the Aquarian is such a strong individualist—living totally by personal standards, and therefore being more completely tolerant of others.

Travel tastes are equally varied. The Aquarian fits in well with people from different surroundings, and finds out about them rather than talking exclusively about his own home base. An Aquarian will try anything once—a camel ride, alligator meat, or the local soft drink. Zest combined with an avid sense of curiosity adds up to many good trips if you are an Aquarian.

HOME AND FAMILY

You love your home even if you are not in it as much as people from other signs. You always want a corner of your own to come back to, and you look forward to seeing your family even if you are rarely homesick in the acute sense.

Because your sense of privacy is so strong, you prefer to have your own room, if possible. Certainly you want some peaceful place where you can be alone.

Wherever this is, you decorate it in your own way, adding creative touches and, most likely, strong, unusual colors. If your taste was not so intuitively good, the results would clash. But you blend elements deftly, in a way that is both unusual and traditionally pleasing.

Your relations with other family members are smooth for the most part. That's because you are self-contained and helpful, and like to "do it yourself." Loud, angry quarrels jar your Aquarian sense of composure, so you generally hold your tongue rather than lose your temper.

But sometimes you should speak up. You may nurse a grievance out of all proportion. Moreover, if you don't tell your parents your troubles, they may think you are being difficult or moody when something is really bothering you.

Your family life will run a little more smoothly when you learn to ask for help when needed, and when you become less oversensitive to criticism. You also occasionally balk at being pushed, but any slight is usually in your own thoughts and was not intended.

You enjoy any brothers and sisters thoroughly—as long as they let you have some peaceful times alone. And you almost always have at least one pet.

FRIENDSHIP

You make the best friends of any of the signs. And you are loyal, and keep close friends for years, frequently for life. (You also keep their secrets and confidences.)

On the other hand, you are not an easy person to get to know well. It takes a long time. Even though you are pleasant and amiable at a first meeting, your deeper qualities come to the fore only after you have warmed to a person. In the beginning you are more shy than truly stand-offish.

You always think the best of a friend, and occasionally seem to let someone walk over you—but eventually you do get angry. And even though you may not say it at first, you hate being imposed upon.

On the other hand, no one is a more generous friend than you are. You will give away anything you have, and you know the real meaning of sharing. Moreover, your friends are of all types and have widely differing opinions, interests, and backgrounds.

You like your friends as they are, even if

you do not always agree with them. Brother-hood and mutual respect are your friendship bywords. And you live by them in all your relationships, from casual to close.

ROMANCE

You are your own person, even in romance. Your nature is both restless and constant. You are always looking for love, and are likely to play the field. You enjoy blind dates and a new face always arouses your curiosity. Sometimes you seem to be more in love with love than with a particular person.

But that is only because you haven't yet found the right person. Once you find the person you are looking for (and your ideals are high), you will be constant. Your romantic restlessness will be replaced by a deep feeling of fulfillment. You are warmly affectionate and have the capacity for great happiness.

But unless you are really serious, you may at times seem a little distant or cold. You don't like to be pinned down, and so you withhold something of yourself. This doesn't mean that you are really cold or aloof. It's just that you don't feel entirely free with the other person.

This can baffle dates, who think you are one

sort when you are really another, down deep. You are such a good sport and pleasant person that you go along with most anything and fit into any situation. You adapt so well that the other person thinks you are in closer harmony than you really are. And occasionally you fool yourself—getting into romantic situations you later find it difficult to get out of.

However, your casual dates and companionable relationships are quite different from your real loves. You have few of these, but when you do, you are totally dedicated and likely to be fiercely possessive. You are completely responsive, and will be heartbroken if anything goes wrong or a third person enters the scene —which rarely happens.

The Aquarian male needs emotional room. He can't stand to be hemmed in or tied down, or to be constantly asked to show how much he cares. Such petty demands will drive him away fast.

Most often he falls for someone who lets him keep his freedom. And then, of course, he loses it—but willingly. When this happens, he is one of the most completely giving and caring of all types. He is thoughtful yet exciting, and his romantic attention seldom strays.

Aquarian females are equally sensitive and thoroughly responsive—when they are with someone who sparks their interest deeply. When they are with someone they care less strongly about, they are good sports and delightful companions, but may seem more sisterly than romantic. And nothing can persuade them but their own personal feelings. An Aquarian female is only true to another when she is true to herself, and she may break many hearts on the path to finding genuine love. But find it she will, eventually.

COMPATIBILITY GUIDE

WITH ARIES: You respond warmly to each other and have much in common. Because you both are so independent, you may want to go off in different directions from time to time. But with a few minor adjustments there is the chance of an exceptionally exciting and happy relationship.

WITH TAURUS: Imagination is what brings the two of you together. You are both tender-hearted and creative, and you see only the good and beautiful in each other. The relationship will be close to ideal, as long as disillusionment doesn't set in. There's always the danger, however, of that crash to reality that could shatter your close harmony.

WITH GEMINI: A lot of outside interests, plus the same leisure and intellectual likes make you seek each other out. You are both Air signs, and you have the further bond of being equally many-sided, energetic types. But Gemini must curb his or her too-quick tongue if the relationship is to realize its fine potential.

WITH CANCER: Cancer will bring out the loving qualities of Aquarius. Aquarius, on the other hand, will provide Cancer with goals and a needed spur to action. These two are likely to be the answer to each other's daydreams—as long as neither becomes sarcastic or critical.

WITH LEO: Who will dominate is the big question between you. But the attraction is powerful, almost magnetic, and you will probably have a stormy but fascinating relationship. Both of you may feel annoyed or depressed at times, but you will never be bored. And you will probably work out any differences.

WITH VIRGO: There may be moments of irritation when Virgo points out the errors of Aquarius' more easygoing ways. On the other hand, Aquarius could perhaps profit by the advice, and if it is given with love, there shouldn't be too much strain on your relationship, which has a lot going for it.

WITH SCORPIO: Sensitivity is the key word here. Yours will be an emotional, almost intuitive relationship. Sometimes you can almost read each other's minds. Scorpio is possessive and could be jealous of Aquarius' many outside interests, but you are so tuned in to each other, you should be able to talk out any minor snags.

WITH LIBRA: Yours is a partnership sort of relationship. You have a great camaraderie as well as a strong mutual attraction. Moreover, you are strong for the same causes. Ideals of justice and sympathy for suffering move you deeply—and into the appropriate action. You balance and bring out the best in each other.

WITH SAGITTARIUS: You both have many interests, and most of them are in common. And you both like the same kind of friends—all kinds, that is. There should be a close, happy togetherness. You excite and respond to each other with zest and affection. Your absorption is likely to be total. It might even be lasting.

WITH CAPRICORN: Despite temperamental differences (Capricorn a planner and Aquarius impulsive), you strongly attract and bring out the best in each other. Capricorn gives this relationship its sense of security, while Aquarius adds the fun.

WITH AQUARIUS: You may have so many friends and interests in common that you never fully develop your own relationship. It is most likely to be companionable, and neither one of you may want to give up your freedom. You both value peace and harmony so highly that together you tend to be lukewarm rather than excited.

WITH PISCES: The affection here is deep, but there may be a problem in expressing it, especially with Pisces, who is intense but withdrawn in showing emotion. The relationship between you is likely to grow, and warm, slowly. The final result should be fulfilling and exceptionally happy.

PISCES

★ *February 19 - March 20* ★

ELEMENT: *Water*
RULED BY: *Neptune*
SYMBOL: *Fish*
KEY WORD: *Sensitive*
JEWEL: *Pearl*
COLORS: *Blue, Green, Pearl Gray;*
Indefinite Shades
LUCKY NUMBER: *7*
LUCKY DAY: *Thursday*

OTHER IMPORTANT PISCEANS:
Elizabeth Taylor
Michelangelo
Rudolph Nureyev
Zero Mostel
Harry Belafonte
Joanne Woodward
Jerry Lewis
Nat "King" Cole
Albert Einstein
Jackie Gleason
Frédéric Chopin
Sidney Poitier
Anthony Armstrong-Jones
John Steinbeck

PISCES

GENERAL CHARACTERISTICS

You are most responsive. Sympathy for others underlies everything you do. You are an emotional person, and are more quiet then fiery by temperament. A Pisces may brood and become moody or feel sorry for himself, but a Pisces almost never rants or yells or loses his temper.

In other words, you are inner-directed. You feel things keenly and you see life through your own idealism and imagination. It actually hurts you to think about war and poverty and tragic happenings. And the minor misfortunes of friends and family affect you deeply.

Pisces' symbol, the Fish, looks both forward and backward. And this is typical of your nature, which is always looking into the future in a prophetic, almost mystic, way—while, on the other hand, being drawn toward the security of tradition and the past.

Serenity is important to you, and you prefer to compromise rather than fight back. Most of the time this is a good thing. You adjust and adapt to all situations and rarely cause trouble or create a scene. But sometimes accommodation is not a constructive thing. You may lapse into laziness or shirk responsibility by doing nothing—as when you let someone take advantage of you or get involved with something the gang does against your own will and better judgment.

You have many fine traits. You are caring, considerate, warm-hearted, and good-tempered. You are also gentle and somewhat spiritual in your response to life.

But you are not sure of yourself. Your greatest lack is of self-confidence. It is hard for you to muster up the courage to fight back or stand up for yourself. Once in a while you think circumstances are against you when in reality you are against yourself. Even when you have everything going for you, you tend to look on the dark side and feel that the good can't possibly last.

But because you have such a generous spirit and are so likeable, good things do abound in your life. People trust you and confide in you and give you the encouragement and slight positive push you need. When you waver, others urge you to act, and this gives you the confidence that rounds you out and makes your Pisces personality bloom.

PHYSICAL CHARACTERISTICS

You are not as robust as some other signs, but you have natural good health, and if you are ill, you respond quickly to treatment.

Two things are important: that you get plenty of exercise (fight flab and fatigue at the same time) and plenty of rest. And it is a good idea for you to stay away from other people who are ill. You are so impressionable, you are likely to take on their physical troubles, or to fret and worry.

Physically, Pisceans are likely to have small bones and exceptionally fine feet and hands. Pisces females frequently have an ethereal, almost mystical, look. Their hair is likely to be flowing and their eyes large and a little dreamy. Pisces males have a slightly mysterious though very masculine appearance.

In clothing, it is important not to be a copy cat. Because you are somewhat unsure of your own taste (which is intuitively sound), you too frequently follow the latest fad or your best friend's fashion advice, which won't help you realize your own unique potential. Wear what you like and instinctively feel good in. This is likely to be a blending of pale, pearly colors and bright accents, of traditional and mod— and should suit you perfectly.

SCHOOL AND CAREER

You have varied talents and leanings in many directions. And you do excellently in subjects requiring imagination.

However, you are not consistent. You sometimes find it hard to concentrate, and detailed facts bore you. Nor are you good at memorizing.

You are likely, for instance, to get excellent grades in English on creative papers but poor ones on tests requiring a thorough knowledge of the rules of composition. And while the romance of history appeals to you, you never can remember a date.

You seem to lack method in doing your homework, but you have a knack for remembering the important point in a lecture and in absorbing the information that counts in a quiz. Your intuition allows you to take short cuts, so often you do better than those who work harder. In fact, you almost always do well in school, except for the occasional times when you get discouraged.

Pisceans are equally successful in their careers. They have a special pull toward jobs requiring imagination and intuition. And they can absorb and express the ideas of others, which often leads them into careers in advertising, publishing, and teaching. And because

Pisces people love to take care of others, many doctors and nurses are born under this sign.

Pisces males are creative and exceptionally gifted salesmen. Set design, commercial art, and religion are other natural interests. The Pisces male also has a flair for engineering and architecture.

Pisces females are all "born actresses," so many are drawn into this profession. They are also apt to make their mark in designing, sculpture, and the cosmetics field. Many part-time poets, musicians, and fine-art painters are born under this sign.

Both Pisces males and females are unusually gifted in creative work, but they should learn to "toot their own horns" a little more.

MONEY

YOUR emotions rule you where money is concerned. You tend to buy on impulse and spend on the spur of the moment. And occasionally you make foolish loans, to friends who can't easily pay you back—which always creates problems. Also, it is hard for you to turn anybody—or any charity—down. You are a frequent financial target because it is so easy to get your sympathy.

On the other hand, you have unusually good luck concerning money. Your financial intuition is excellent. When you have a hunch about a project, or later in life about an investment, it almost always pays off.

Because you more than others need a sense of security, it is important that you have some savings put aside. Lack of funds worries you. You are generous, and you like nice things, so it may be difficult for you to save. But it is important that you try.

FUN AND LEISURE

You prefer sports on the quiet side—walking, swimming, fishing, and sailing. You have an almost mystical feeling about nature and thoroughly enjoy camping and mountain climbing. You feel emotionally attuned to trees, lakes, and windswept hills.

In books, art, and records, your tastes are typical of your Fish symbol. You see both backwards and forwards, and like equally the old and the new. Shakespeare and Mailer, Bach and the Beatles, Rembrandt and pop art—all appeal to you.

Your collections reflect the same duality. Your weaknesses might be for antique cups and mod posters. And you love to rummage through thrift shops, book stalls, and old coin stores.

Your party preference is for small, intimate gatherings. Even just one other special soul mate is enough for you to feel festive. Your scene includes plenty of atmosphere—flowers and candlelight and soft music. Your wit is subtle and your voice generally soft. You like to entertain, and know how to make people feel happy and emotionally at home.

You like to take trips, but prefer short jaunts to being away from home base for long periods. Frequently, you travel through your imagination, by reading and going to movies and hearing about other places and people. And whether really there or not, you completely enter into the spirit of your temporary surroundings.

HOME AND FAMILY

YOUR surroundings mean more to you than to people born under other signs. You must live in harmony to feel whole. More than others, you want a place where you can relax.

You need quiet, and you like to see things in order. Anger and noise make you feel jumpy, and when your room is disorganized, you feel that way too.

Any family bickering and the loud voices of younger brothers and sisters can get on your nerves. You dislike disturbances so much that occasionally you don't stick up for your own rights. If you have older brothers and sisters who were born under Fire signs (Aries, Leo, and Sagittarius), they may unthinkingly dominate the household and usurp the biggest and best. Rather than become moody and resentful, you must learn to talk out the problem, and to stand up for your rights.

Even with your parents, you are sometimes too amiable and agreeable. Underneath you want your own way, but you don't know quite how to ask for it. Simply put, it is hard for you to be aggressive in family affairs. You tend to mask your true thoughts and feelings.

Sensitivity is what causes you to put up this smoke screen. Moreover, you value peace and are such an idealist that it is hard for you to admit to momentary hostility or anger. Eventually, you feel misunderstood, which is mostly a lack of self-confidence on your part.

Fortunately, your parents not only care for you deeply but can usually figure you out better than you think. They know how to shake you out of these infrequent spells of conflict and self-pity by giving you large doses of love and encouragement and by urging you to take a more positive stand.

FRIENDSHIP

You are an ideal friend because you have great empathy for others. Emotionally, you can put yourself in a friend's place and sense things from his or her viewpoint. Your sympathy is active and you have excellent intuition.

You are sensitive; sometimes too sensitive. You may imagine slights where none were intended, and you can be deeply wounded by careless words. When you are hurt, you tend to brood and become moody. Action is the best cure for these occasional bouts of gloomy introspection. Communicating your feeling will also help. Let "Do, don't stew" be your motto whenever minor misunderstandings arise.

On the plus side, your sensitivity makes you warm and affectionate and caring. You are a good listener and you feel deeply about the troubles of others. People love to confide in you and occasionally cry on your shoulder. Your perception is keen and your heart compassionate.

You are loyal to your friends—all of them—but sometimes you lose yourself in trying to please others. Friends like you for what you are, not for being like them. They won't respect you any the less if you disagree or speak your own piece.

You will do anything for a friend, and what you need most from friends in return is encouragement. You are only shy and indecisive when you are unsure of yourself. Luckily, you usually have many close, caring friends who want you to believe in yourself as much as they believe in you.

ROMANCE

You are an emotional person who needs affection. Your heart definitely rules your head and feeling is all-important to you. Good, "sensible" reasons never influence your romantic decisions; "I feel" completely outweighs "I think."

Sensitivity is the key to your romantic nature. You need constant reassurance that the one you care for cares for you in return. You are possessive, and the slightest flirtation on his or her part wounds you and worries you all out of proportion. Sometimes you are hurt much too easily, and suspicion can mar your relationships.

Moreover, you are such a dreamer and such an idealist that you may not see the object of your affections as he or she really is. You tend to romanticize, and are then disillusioned when the one you care about turns out to be less than perfect. You would do better not to put the object of your affection on such a high pedestal in the first place.

You rarely oppose the interests or ideas of your dates. You blend in, and sometimes say "yes" when you really mean "no." You have the courage of your convictions, but it's hard for you to wound another person's feelings. You may end up leading someone on—not intentionally, but simply because you don't know how to get out of the situation. In such cases, it is best to be honest, even if it is hard.

You tend to have many love interests, and occasionally get crushes on people you hardly know. But you have few serious romances, and they are almost always with strong-spirited partners who free your affection by making you believe in yourself.

Romantically, you are one of the most receptive of all the signs. And you are one of the most sentimental and thoughtful. You will do anything—changing your hair-do, growing sideburns, or running an errand—for your loved one.

The Pisces male is easily made jealous. But he is one of the least selfish and most sentimental of dates. Also, he is extremely sympathetic and loves to hear how his date feels.

Because he is so emotional, he can be moody at times, and his feelings can be hurt easily.

You can't respond too warmly or tell him too often how much you care.

The Pisces female also needs frequent reassurances about love. Actions may be stronger than words, but words and romantic gestures mean more to her. She is not very practical and she is never calculating.

She is more timid than other types and rarely takes the romantic lead. But while she is not aggressive, she is always considerate, sensitive, and sincere—which makes her an ideal partner in romance.

COMPATIBILITY GUIDE

WITH ARIES: Sometimes fiery, strong-willed Aries comes on too strong for shy, sensitive Pisces. But, on the other hand, you are good for each other and strongly attracted. Because you are both so romantic, you are likely to bridge the gap between temperamental differences and be delightfully happy.

WITH TAURUS: Any courtship would take a long time, since you are both slow in getting started. (And you might each be waiting for the other to make the first move.) But once you get together, the relationship should be a warm one that keeps on growing. You should give each other great joy.

WITH GEMINI: Gemini is a sensitive soul who can understand Pisces' moods better than most. You have a lot in common and should be responsive to each other's deepest desires and ideals. But will-o'-the-wisp Gemini should try not to make Pisces jealous. The resulting hurt feelings could seriously strain your otherwise good relationship.

WITH CANCER: You are both intuitive and a lot alike. And you are both super-sensitive, which could bring you closely together or be a bone of contention, resulting in moodiness and long silent spells. Communication is the most important key word here. Talk out any problems, and be as kind and considerate as you are affectionate.

WITH LEO: Leo could overpower Pisces, and drive him or her deeply into a shell of shyness. But because you are so strongly drawn toward each other, the outcome is likely to be positive. Dramatic, zestful Leo is likely to bring joy and self-confidence into Pisces' life. And Pisces, in turn, will somewhat temper Leo's roaming nature.

WITH VIRGO: You blend nicely, but the relationship may be more companionable than exciting. Virgo will protect Pisces from the harsher aspects of reality and Pisces will add warmth to Virgo's practicality. Even if you eventually break up, you will probably remain good friends.

WITH LIBRA: You both have a strong artistic bent, but Libra approaches romance from a mental-plus-emotional attitude while Pisces approaches it from pure feeling. If quarrels develop, Libra might accuse Pisces of being too emotional, while Pisces could rightly accuse Libra of being unsentimental and somewhat cold. You will both have to make adjustments to make this twosome a success.

WITH SCORPIO: You both care about the little things, and should have an exciting if not always smooth time getting to know each other. You are both warm-hearted and deeply responsive, and even ordinary occasions like walking to school or stopping for a pizza can turn into romantic occasions.

WITH SAGITTARIUS: You harmonize, and have a rapport that should bridge any differences in temperament. (Sagittarius is more social and outgoing, while Pisces is shy and inner-directed.) In fact, you attract each other because you are *not* alike. Mutual curiosity should lead you into an exciting relationship.

WITH CAPRICORN: Practical Capricorn may not always sympathize with Pisces' feelings. And Pisces could possibly end the relationship abruptly if his or her feelings become too deeply wounded. The best way to avoid this is to discuss differences before they turn into real rifts. Affection and compromise are important on both sides.

WITH AQUARIUS: You are both idealistic and imaginative. But Aquarius' many interests might cause Pisces to feel neglected, and Pisces might expect more of a commitment than freedom-loving Aquarius is willing to make. The forecast is positive only if both care deeply—and more about each other's feelings than their own.

WITH PISCES: Both of you feel strongly and the same way about many things, which could lead to mutual moodiness, or to soul-close sympathy and understanding. There is a slightly explosive quality to your relationship. You must be constantly careful and considerate, but the joy you find together should be worth the effort.